WILD HORSES

WILD HORSES
IN MY
BLOOD

BY EVA PENDLETON HENDERSON

SUNSTONE
PRESS

SANTA FE

This book was published orginally in 1983 as *WILD HORSES*.

Sunstone books may be purchased for educational, business, or sales promotional
use. For information please write: Special Markets Department, Sunstone Press, P.O.
Box 2321, Santa Fe, New Mexico 87504-2321.

NEW EDITION

10 9 8 7 6 5 4 3 2 1

Library of Congress Cataloging-in-Publication Data:

Henderson, Eva Pendleton, 1890–
[Wild horses]
Wild horses in my blood / by Eva Pendleton Henderson.--New ed.
      p.cm
Originally published: Wild horses. 1983.
ISBN: 0-86534-336-5
      1. Henderson, Eva Pendleton, 1890----Childhood and youth.
2. Frontier and pioneer life--New Mexico. 3. Ranchers--New Mexico--Biography.
4. New Mexico--Social life and customs. 5. New Mexico--Biography. I. Title.

CT275.H558 A3 2001
978.9'4204'092--dc21
[B]   2001034221

Published in   SUNSTONE PRESS
                   Post Office Box 2321
                   Santa Fe, NM 87504-2321 / USA
                   (505) 988-4418 / *orders only* (800) 243-5644
                   FAX (505) 988-1025
                   www.sunstonepress.com

CONTENTS

Eva Pendleton Henderson

FOREWORD

This narrative is set in the territorial days of New Mexico beginning in the year 1895.

It is authentic. I know because I lived it.

We lived on the ragged edge of life. My family was clean and fine, poor and proud. We rode wagons or saddle horses. Our schooling was scarce, but our lives were rich with experiences.

Let me tell you how it was.

Eva Pendleton Henderson

PART ONE

CHAPTER ONE

WILD HORSES

The hot sun looks like a mesquite fire low in the west. The mesquite bushes that grow all around cast sketchy shadows on the bleached walls of the tent we live in. To me, the shadows appear like marching nomads. I open the tent flaps which serve as a door and look out over the prairie. The two milk cows, grazing toward the brush corral where their calves are penned, break the prairie stillness with their soft lowing.

I hear thundering hooves and see plumes of dust rising into the sky made by the bunch of stock horses which Papa and my 12-year-old brother, Holland, are driving to camp.

When you corral a bunch of ranch horses, one rider gets in the lead and stays there, while the other rides herd until the entire bunch are following the leader.

Papa is riding Jingle-Bob, a stray, but dandy piece of horse-flesh. He has maneuvered Jingle-Bob to the lead of the bunched wild horses and Holland, riding a sorrel gelding named Rebel and branded E (our horse brand) is following close behind. Rebel, colt of Red Cloud, is a thoroughbred owned by my brother and is the best bred horse on the range. Holland looks like a young Indian as he rides with ease and grace among the herd.

Papa heads straight for the corral gate. The wild horses, tails and manes fanned into the air, follow into the corral where the stallion Red Cloud suddenly realizes that he and his mares are trapped. Standing on his hind feet he paws the air, the sun glistening on his sides, his keen angry whinny sounding like a bugle in the dry air.

Papa leads Jingle-Bob from the corral and drops the bridle reins to the ground, Holland does the same with Rebel. Then Papa takes his rope from the saddle, makes a loop and straight as an arrow pitches it around the neck of a young bay gelding, a beauty, one of Red Cloud's colts.

During the corraling of the horses I stood quietly by the tent wall. Now I run to the gate and Papa says quietly, "Eva, open the gate and stand behind it."

The horses stream out of the corral and head for the open prairie. The young bay fights the rope as the others leave but soon Papa and Holland have him hackamored and saddled and when Holland gets aboard him, the bay really lets loose, bucking and bawling. Holland sticks like a burr—and every time the young bay bucks, Holland rakes with his spurs.

Then comes the clear musical ring of the cowbell. Mama's call to supper.

Sourdough biscuits, jerky, cream gravy, lick (that's molasses), butter and a cup of milk, the cup made from a small tin can. Gingerly I take a sip of milk, fearful that it is *blue Johnny* or maybe tastes of onions. But it is delicious buttermilk.

Blue Johnny milk is the stage called *blinkie* just before the milk goes sour. As to my other apprehension—wild onions— they appear after a prairie rain and give the milk a distinct strong taste.

After supper Papa reaches into a box beneath the bed. I know what comes next. He brings out our old worn spelling book. I hope he sticks to the words in the book instead of ones he likes that come from Mexico, words like "Oaxaca," "Zacatecas." Even worse he might go far north and hit us with something like "Massachusetts." These hard words remind me of the large discarded tree chunks left in the wood pile, too tough to chop. But we are lucky tonight and the spelling lesson is short and easy.

Papa appears tired. Mama blows out the coal-oil lamp and we go to bed.

Late in the night I hear a commotion outside the tent—the neighing and screaming of a horse in pain.

Jingle-Bob plunges through the tent door which Papa always leaves open and in the clear moonlight his teeth are glaring whitely, ears laid back, his eyes look like red balls of fire.

Papa's vocabulary of curse words would reach from hell to breakfast. Jingle-Bob backs out of the tent and runs screaming back to the open range.

Papa sits on the side of the bed, head bowed, face in hands. From my bed I can see moonlight shining on his head, teardrops trickling through his work-stained fingers. His sigh seems to come all the way up from his toes.

"That horse is crazy," Mama says.

"Yes," Papa says, "and begging for help. It is a case of acute colic. He'll die before morning."

Mama says, "You couldn't save him."

"No, and the sad thing is, I'm out of the colic medicine. I'll send the wagon to Eddy tomorrow for supplies and turpentine."

Next morning Jingle-Bob is dead.

We bow our heads and ask God to find pasturage for Jingle-Bob, adding a note of instruction for his care and feeding: "God," we say, "he likes mesquite beans."

But Papa adds, "He ate too many ripe mesquite beans. That's what gave him the colic."

Dust clouds rise in the east and west. We see two bunches of horses, the black Kemp stallion and Red Cloud, our stallion, driving their harems of mares to water. The studs circle the mares, trot along beside or behind them.

We do not go near the lake. Wild stallions are dangerous, especially in Spring.

When the mares come to the edge of the lake and start drinking Red Cloud whinnies, backs his ears and runs at the black stallion. The black rears, too, paws the air and they both go up on their hind feet pawing at each other. Fierce snorts and keen whinnies fill the morning air. Red Cloud bites the black on the shoulder, then quick as a flash he whirls and kicks him. The black backs off, Red Cloud lopes to the mares, thinking he has him beaten, but the black darts up beside Red Cloud, whirls and kicks him on the hind leg. The sound is like a shot. Red Cloud falls to the ground. The black proudly circles both bunches of mares and heads for the foothills.

We run to tell Papa. He and the boys are digging a well near the tent.

Red Cloud struggles to get up, but his leg hangs, useless, and my father and the boys build a scaffold to raise him up. His proud head is bent low to the ground. On the third day after the fight, he still refuses to eat and Papa goes to visit Red Cloud early in the morning with his 45 six shooter in his hand.

Quietly I follow behind. Papa raises the gun and aims between the horse's eyes. He squeezes the trigger, bows his head and bursts into tears.

"Goddammit, Red Cloud," he cries, "I had to do it. But Goddamn that black son of a bitch! I'd like to kill him too!"

I reach out and take Papa's hand.

"Papa, let's go and kill that black son of a bitch."

Papa takes a red bandanna from his pocket, wipes his eyes and blows his nose. Then he looks me in the face and says,

"Never use those or any cuss words again. Do you hear?"

"Yes, Papa." Then I help him unloose the scaffold and lower Red Cloud to the ground.

No one ever rode Red Cloud but Papa and I knew that tears are still dropping from his heart, though he carefully keeps them from his eyes.

Summer fades into fall. The days grow cold, we burn mesquite roots for warmth.

CHAPTER TWO

BUBBLING SPRINGS

The little town of Eddy is nestled on the banks of the Pecos River. The streets are lined with mesquite bushes with a few cottonwood trees here and there to give shade to the town. We use mesquite roots for cooking and heating and occasionally cow chips for the cook stoves; and although they produce only a little heat, at least they have no odor.

Clear rippling springs bubble from the banks of the Pecos River and are compared to the famous health waters of Carlsbad, Germany. To me a drink from these springs is a stiff dose of Epsom salts; however, the water is bottled in five gallon containers and shipped east and west on the railroad. Coffee made of this spring water looks beautiful, but the taste is predictably bad.

Papa trades horses for a windmill, for milk cows and for many other things. Money is scarce.

My brothers Dick and Jack grub mesquite roots for fuel, both for selling and using at home. Mama has a list written on a piece of paper torn from a brown paper bag and I watch the pile of mesquite wood grow higher and her list of groceries and other necessities grow longer and longer.

Later on Dick and Jack are hired to ride a trail herd to Amarillo, Texas. Gathering and driving a large herd of cattle so far is a tough job and the boys are away for over two months. But after the cattle herd is paid for and loaded on the train, the boss and all of the cowboys ride into the city and Jack meets our uncle, Jeff Chisum.

Uncle Jeff is so delighted to see Jack he buys him a very expensive saddle which immediately replaces Jack's beat-up old one. With great pride Jack cinches the new saddle on Panzone, his pony, and rides back into camp.

"Where'd you get such a fine saddle?" Dick says when he first lays his eyes on it. The moment he hears the story, Dick takes off for Amarillo on Black Bess, his own mount, but though he looks everywhere he is out of luck because Uncle Jeff and his men left town soon after Jack did.

Back at home the woodpile is very high and the list of groceries is longer than before. Papa and Holland, my other brother, have loaded a great pile of wood on the wagon.

That night we eat a supper of mush and milk. We can smell the perfume of the last wildflowers as we sit and eat near the tent door.

In the morning we are up early, Holland rustling the wagon team, Lee and Grant—I'm Southern so I put Lee first. Holland finds a beautiful little bird with a broken wing and gives it to me for a present. Papa sets the bird's wing, bracing it with half of a kitchen match but he refuses to let me have the bird for a pet.

"Turn the bird loose," he says sternly. "Never make a captive of bird or beast unless it is absolutely necessary."

Thinking of the proud high-stepping pony that fought so bravely for his freedom only a few days before, I say,

"Papa—when *is* it necessary?"

Papa is not what I'd call a churchgoer, but he answers, "In the book of Genesis it is written that God gave man dominion. You learn when and how to exercise your God given dominion."

It is a lesson I never forget.

Late the next afternoon I imagine hearing the rumble of wagon wheels. Placing my ear flat on the earth, I distinctly hear wagon wheels and the sound of horses' hooves. It's Holland coming back from town. When I run out to meet him I see a small baby sitting next to him on the wagon seat! Lee and Grant hang their heads, tired and jaded. And Holland bursts out laughing because it's not a baby beside him on the wagon seat, it is the largest doll I have ever seen.

"Martin Marose's little girl sends it to you," he says.

I've never seen Martin Marose's little girl, and yet she is sending me my first doll! I can't believe it. Later that day Papa drives a nail in the center pole of the tent and he ties my lovely doll to it. The doll's long eyelashes cast lacy shadows on her pink cheeks and I sit down and stare at her admiringly. From the tent pole, out of the way, she can't be stepped on or hurt.

While I am loving my first doll, Papa asks Holland a serious question.

"Did Martin Marose make it across the border into Mexico?"

Holland nods yes.

"Dave Kemp said to tell you. Mr. Kemp also said to tell you that no sheriff in the territory could have overtaken Martin mounted on either of those horses he got from you."

A couple of nights before, Martin came to see Papa late in the evening. Martin was up to something, but Papa traded him horses for his cattle, March 15, 1895.

Later we hear that Martin is killed by a man who is supposed to be his friend. This friend writes and asks Martin to meet him on the bridge over the Rio Grande River between the United States and Mexico. Martin meets the fellow and he is shot and killed. Holland says, "Martin Marose slapped rope and brand on a few unbranded calves and that's where it got him."

Papa raises and sells good horses and in these early territorial days of New Mexico it is considered a worse crime to steal a horse than a cow. Stealing a horse is a hanging offense.

Hundreds of horses and cattle roam the country. There are no drift fences.

We are camped near a very large lake which never seems to go dry. Cattle drift from southwest Texas and water at this lake and sometimes cattle come to where our wash is hung and chew our clothes. We hang our wash on mesquite bushes and the hungry cattle come and chew anything hanging on the bushes that has the taste of salt.

Some of the cattle wear the brand LFD—Left for Dead. According to legend, when cattle were too weak and water too scarce, the Chisum cowboys would abandon the ones that couldn't make it.

Big unbranded yearlings are also around the lake. They are

called mavericks, and we are always excited and happy to find one. Our brand is 2N2 on the left side. The 2 is on shoulder and hip and the N on the side. Our horse brand is E͜ called *E rocker.*

All the cowboys carry a running iron on their saddles. I learn how to write with one of these branding irons.

The season rolls on, the mesquite beans are gone. Only a few grotesque hulls dangle from the limbs of the mesquite bushes. Some of the shadows of those beans remind me of a man being hanged from a tree limb. A Mr. Garrett is hanged in Eddy one year, I think it is in 1894, and school is dismissed that day...

But now the days grow colder and glide into winter. Papa seems worried. The well is not finished, the tent walls are paper thin.

CHAPTER THREE

SON OF A GUN

Mama rings the cowbell loud and clear and the sound drifts way across the prairie. You could smell what we were having for supper—"Son of a gun" with golden brown sourdough biscuits.

I pass my plate and say, as Mama taught us, "If you please, give me a helping of the son of a gun."

Mama stops filling plates, holding her spoon in mid-air.

"What did you say, Miss?"

When Mama is provoked at me she always calls me "Miss."

I hurriedly correct myself.

"If you please, give me a helping of the stew-boil-fry."

When Mama levels at me what I later called the "Chisum look," I wilt. Mama was a Chisum. It was the cowpunchers who got me in trouble by naming this delicious dish S.O.B. They named it after a certain sheriff whom they disliked and distrusted and whose name I won't bother to mention.

My sister Clara is beautiful and gracious. When the wild flowers are in bloom she always gathers a bouquet and keeps them on the kitchen table. The flower arrangement is in a large tomato can, but it gives our table a fiesta look.

The seats of our wooden chairs are covered with rawhide.

One day Dave Kemp came to court my lovely sister Clara. He is the first Sheriff of Eddy, New Mexico, and he is a gambler, tough as a boot-heel. On the little finger of his left hand he has a great big diamond ring. Dave is handsome, polite. His voice is soft and clear and unaffected.

Papa wears the pants at our house, mostly, and he likes Dave Kemp, mostly. But this morning Mama is in command.

"Mr. Kemp," she calls across the yard. "you are not to come

to see Clara any more. Take that horse back with you too."

Her eyes flash fire—not at Mr. Kemp, at Papa, who is gazing out over the wide open spaces.

Mr. Kemp speaks directly to Mama.

"Mrs. Bass, I bought this horse for Clara."

Then he turns the pony loose and his eyes sparkle like the rays from the diamond ring he is wearing. I sneak a quick look at his face; it reminds me of a wild prairie fire.

Dave walks up to Clara, boldly takes her hand, leads her to where his horse is standing, a black horse with silver mountings on the saddle. He talks softly for a few moments with Clara. He is holding her hand the whole time. Then he stoops and kisses her on the forehead, mounts his shining black horse and rides off toward Eddy.

Clara names her new pony David.

Several years before that day, Dave Kemp was arrested in Texas on a charge of murder. At the trial, the courthouse window is open and a friend of Dave's saddles and ties his horse near the courthouse window. The window is several feet from the ground on the second floor of the courthouse.

When Dave is brought into the courtroom, the evidence appears convincing; Dave is in deep trouble. There is much excitement in the courtroom. During the confusion, Dave runs to the open window and leaps to the ground where he breaks his ankle, yet he hops into the saddle and manages to ride off helter skelter. Dave, "on the dodge" comes to the territory of New Mexico. Many of the first settlers of the territory were dodging the law.

We never hear from Dave again, but my sister never forgot the day he brought her gift pony.

Colonel Benson and his son Hollie come to see Papa one day. Mama tells us to go to the lake and make mud horses. She gives us some jerky to take with us.

The bottom of the lake is red clay from which we make roses, horses and cattle and set them to dry beneath the big mesquite bushes.

Colonel Benson ends up buying from Papa the claim on the land we are homesteading. Under Colonel Benson's management, this ranch became the famous TX Ranch, one of the largest in the Southwest.

Colonel Benson's foreman, Lyn Scott is a man among men, six feet seven in his sock feet. I think he looks like a god: golden curly hair, gray eyes, a voice that charms the birds out of the mesquite bushes.

One day Lyn comes courting lovely Clara. Mama likes Lyn Scott. He sings old cowboy songs including *California Joe*, all forty-eight verses and his voice is high as a bugle and soft as the murmur of a mountain stream. I've seen old ladies quietly wipe tears from their eyes when he sings *Little Joe the Wrangler* perhaps because one of their sons or brothers has been killed in a cattle stampede.

I remember a young man who was trampled to death. The herd was camped near Carlsbad on a rainy night and the cowboys were standing night guard when lightning made the herd stampede. I do not recall the boy's name, but he moved his night horse to the lead of this wild bunch of fear-stricken cattle and was trying to get the herd to run in a circle when his horse hit a prairie dog hole, stumbled and fell and the boy was trampled to death. He'd drawn his wages that afternoon, written a letter to his mother saying he was coming home. He was my brother's good friend.

I can't remember his name.

CHAPTER FOUR

BLACK RIVER

Papa trades horses for a place twenty miles south of Eddy, the town they later named Carlsbad.

We are excited and eager to see our new home.

The wagon is being loaded, very early in the morning. The last thing they do is to take down the tent, roll and load it. Brother Holland has already left, driving some cattle, including the milk cows, Pied and Brindle, with their calves. Holland is riding the bay pony that Clara named Handsome Harry.

Papa saddles Toppy and ties him behind the wagon. I ask if I may ride Toppy. Mama says no.

We are ready to leave our home on the prairie. I take one last look at the lake, the water shimmering in the early morning sunlight, the air bright and clear.

The corrals are empty. The tarpaulin has been removed from the four posts. I see a scar on the face of the prairie—the remains of our privy.

The shimmering lake, the vast prairie, may be a bleak picture to some, but to me it spells freedom, home on the range.

Twenty miles is a long day's drive for a team pulling a loaded wagon, so we camp near Eddy. Holland gets permission to put the cattle and horses in a pasture beside our camp site, then he rides into town and brings back sweet potatoes and link sausage for supper. Clara boils the potatoes in a big iron kettle over the campfire and Papa cuts limbs from mesquite bushes and we put the sausages on the thorns of the limbs to broil.

We sit on the ground and eat our supper. The moon is shining in a sky full of stars.

Friends from town come to see us at the campsite and they all sit on the ground with us. Holland keeps the campfire burning brightly. One of the visitors plays *Swanee River* on his French harp. Soon everyone starts to sing. During a breather, I shyly mention that I know all forty-eight verses of *California Joe*. There are no comments.

Then the coyotes begin to howl and the evening is over. Everyone is laughing and saying goodnight and mounting up with the girls riding sideways on men's saddles because few town girls have enough money to buy side saddles.

Papa and Holland roll out the camp beds and we bed down under the stars.

When we break camp early, Clara pours the last of the coffee over the mesquite coals. It is the law of the range not to leave a fire burning.

For lunch Mama gives us some jerky to eat and we chew it on the move. Dark clouds appear overhead and lightning starts to flash; then loud claps of thunder shake the sky and an odor like gun smoke fills the air. A heavy rainstorm starts and stops and hail dances on the wagon top, pelting the cattle so they lower their heads and bawl. I watch the desert lightning play on their shiny wet horns. The team, Grant and Lee, are trying to run, but Papa holds the reins tightly in one hand and keeps his other on the wagon brake. He keeps looking fretfully toward Holland. Then the cattle break and run and the situation worsens. Holland has maneuvered his horse to the side of the running cattle and is trying to get Handsome Harry in the lead of the stampeding herd.

In a low tone Papa says, "Eva, go and help Holland."

Mama screams, "No!"

Papa unties Toppy and helps me climb into the saddle. The stirrups are too long. I put my bare feet between the stirrup leathers and quietly Papa says, "Toppy knows what to do. Turn him toward the herd and stay on."

I turn Toppy in the direction of the cattle and he starts off in a gentle lope which soon turns into a gallop that brings us quickly up to Holland. He has managed to get into his slicker, pulling his hat down over his head. He motions me to follow him and Toppy understands his order. When Holland crowds the leaders to the south, Toppy follows. In a little while the danger is passed and we have them headed toward their new home. The tired cattle drift over the wet prairie like slow moving leaves.

At the top of a ridge we look down into a little valley and see a large house surrounded by trees, a dark flowing river winding its way through trees and more trees. The sun has come out of the dark clouds and gleams on the flowing stream.

What an amazing sight after the bleak tent home on the prairie we so recently left. When the rest of the family arrive, we start exploring and find a lovely orchard, a vineyard and a garden that still has some artichokes—the ones in the ground like potatoes—and a bed of celery and cabbage.

We help unpack and put up the cookstove and straight away Mama fries potatoes, makes cream jerky gravy and light sourdough biscuits served with molasses. A wonderful feast in our new home on Black River.

The town called Black River Village is a large settlement of interesting people, but with no school. Papa and some other men have a meeting to consider the building of a schoolhouse. Some throw in money, others give generously of their time and soon there is a schoolhouse in Black River Village which also serves as a community center. On Friday nights we have spelling bees and once a month, a dance. People come in wagons and on horseback and start dancing at sundown. They do waltzes, polkas, schottisches and square dances—commonly called breakdowns—until dawn. Each family brings a cake.

About ten o'clock the men build a fire and heat a large iron kettle of water into which they pour packages of Arbuckle coffee. I hear Mama say that she thinks the men have hard liquor hidden among the mesquite bushes, since they seem to be jollier after each trip to build up the fire.

One night soon after we have become settled in our new

home, I hear Mama and Holland talking. They are sitting beside the cookstove and I am on the wood box. They are discussing our new neighbor.

Holland says "kinda low-like" to Mama: "Some of these young ladies use tobacco. I'm proud *my* sisters don't."

My face starts to burn.

"I dip snuff," I say. "Lute 'n I've been dippin' since we first moved here."

Mama grabs me by the arm and starts to shake me.

"Where did you get snuff? Are you stealing from me, your own mother?"

"Oh no, Mama. We wouldn't steal from you. We steal from Mrs. Francis."

Mama's anger shows in her eyes. They have the look of cold steel. Suddenly she turns toward the wall, puts her face in her hands and I see her shoulders begin to shake.

"I'll take this up with your father," she says firmly.

Mama is a southern lady, very proud of her heritage, and although she has dipped snuff for many years, she won't be caught dead permitting her daughters to dip.

That night I realize before falling asleep that Mama wasn't crying when she put her face in her hands.

Mama was laughing.

CHAPTER FIVE

WILD TEA

It is planting time. My sister and I are sent to drop the corn and put out the cabbage plants. We drive with Ron Jones, a sod-buster and bee man, in a hack each morning to our field which is three miles from our house. Ron had charge of our bee acre.

Following the plow and putting out the tiny plants is wonderful and the soft loamy dirt feels like velvet under my bare feet.

Ron points to a small greyish plant growing at the edge of the field. "Wild tea," he says, "plumb good to drink."

We gather some, tying it in small bundles with blades of grass and hanging it under the hack bed to dry just as Ron tells us to do. It dries quickly and we have hot tea with our cold lunch.

Come fall the corn is high in the field, the roasting ears are ready to eat. The silk on the ears makes tassels of gold in the sunlight.

My sister and I are sent to the field to bring in the roasting ears. We ride burros. She rides Whitie and I ride Little Blue Jenny —both of us on side saddles.

We see a dust and then two cowboys riding the range.

My sister gets excited because she is sure one of the riders is John, her beau, and she doesn't want to be seen carrying a "towsack" of corn on a burro. We whip and spur Whitie and Little Blue Jenny into what I call a high lope, but Whitie hits a dog hole and my sister and the corn take a spill.

Presently, the two cowboys dash up and dismount. Sure enough, one of them is John. Together they help resack the corn, then John steps up to Whitie and sister daintily lifts her left foot and places it in his hand. John swings her into the saddle. My sister whispers, "Don't tell about Whitie falling; if you do you can't go with me any more."

I promise.

One beautiful cool Saturday morning I decide to go riding with my sister Clara and her beau Lyn Scott. The night before Lyn had ridden in from the TX ranch, our old home, forty miles east of Black River. So I saddle Toppy and ride out toward the river to join them. Lyn turns his horse and rides up beside me, hands me a nickel from his pocket and says, "Get lost."

I turn Toppy and ride away.

Later in the day Lyn and Papa have a serious talk; he asks for Clara's hand in marriage and Papa gives his consent.

In the days that follow, Clara makes her wedding gown, cream cashmere, trimmed in satin and lace.

The wedding ceremony takes place in our home along with the wedding supper—chicken salad, tiny golden brown sourdough biscuits, lots of coffee and a beautiful wedding cake with coconut scattered over it. The cake reminds me of Signal Peak in a snowstorm. Signal is the highest peak in Texas, between Eddy and El Paso.

Among Clara's wedding gifts is a lovely jewel box lined with pink satin. Inside there is a little white card with "Dave Kemp" written on it. Papa gives Clara the high-stepping pony that she had named Handsome Harry.

After supper we go to the school house where friends from all over the county are coming to the "baile." They come from Eddy, Florence, Malaga and ranches near and far. Each family brings a cake and the guests unhitch, unsaddle and hobble their horses while most of the young ladies go behind the schoolhouse to change into their ball dresses. These ball dresses are carried in flour sacks and tied behind their saddles. Some of the girls go farther out behind the high mesquite bushes to change. The high brush also serves as walls for a privy. The girls are shaking out all the wrinkles they can from their ball dresses, pink, yellow and blue, making me think of so many wild flowers.

Clara is beautiful. On the floor she is graceful as a fawn. Lyn Scott is shy, a little awkward on the schoolhouse dance floor.

Professor Griffin plays the fiddle. Once or twice George Pendleton takes the violin and I hear him say kind of low to Professor Griffin, "Go have a little dram of redeye stashed near the coffee."

George Pendleton and his family live north of Eddy on a ranch called the PEN Ranch. He is a fine generous man who signs more notes for friends at the bank than anyone else in the county. To get credit at the bank you have to have someone sign your note. Mr. Pendleton is a wonderful violinist too and he takes first prize at many of the fiddlers' contests.

Clara's wedding makes a great impression on me. The Pendleton family is a part of it.

CHAPTER SIX

THE RAGING PECOS

July and August are the only rainy months in New Mexico, but when the rains come, the wild flowers start to bloom and the hills and plains are a bright carpet of many colors: the Apache plum, sago lily, Indian paintbrush and other wild flowers of the night winds. Cactus comes into bloom early spring to late fall even when there is no rain.

About five miles north of Eddy lies the Avalon Dam and the people who live below it are concerned for their safety during heavy rains because they fear the dam could break.

Steady rain has fallen for days. The Pecos is on a rampage with banks overflowing. The bridge sways on its girder supports and people who live in Eddy abandon their homes and go to the western hills. Several come to our home since we live three miles west of town.

They hurriedly gather their prized possessions, usually tied up in sheets or stuffed into flour sacks and take to the road. We see hordes of frightened people walking with packs on their backs, some in buggies and wagons, fleeing to the safety of the high hills.

They congregate at the bridge north of Eddy where big pieces of timber and other refuse float down the swift river, lodging against the bridge and causing it to sway dangerously.

My two brothers, Holland and Jack, are just returning from the cow-works with a *remuda* of horses. A *remuda* is a group of about seven to ten saddle horses. Papa's saddle horse, Blue Dart, is among them, saddled and bridled with a red and black Navajo saddle blanket.

Jack owns a ranch twenty miles north of Eddy called Lost Ranch. Together my brothers drive their horses to the bridge, hoping to cross. Everyone tells them not to try because it is too risky. The roar of the wild Pecos fills the air.

Jack, who is riding Dogie, a bay thoroughbred and one of Red Cloud's colts, steps from his saddle to tighten the front cinch.

"Holland," he says, "take our saddle horses back. You can't cross this river."

Jack seems bent on accepting the challenge.

Someone on the bank says, "Jack you can't make it. Think of your wife and kids."

Jack says, "My wife and kids are on the other side."

Jack has ridden Dogie in some of the worst cattle stampedes there were; he's a cutting horse and can turn on a penny. Jack mounts him and rides onto the swaying bridge. Leaning forward in the saddle, not touching Dogie with spur or rein, Jack makes it two-thirds of the way across the bridge when one whole section breaks and falls into the river just in front of them.

Dogie stops dead still.

Jack thinks for a moment: Shall we try and jump the span?

The voices on the bank are quiet. Jack touches the reins lightly to the right; Dogie whirls on his hind feet—a picture I'll never forget—and they race back the way they came.

When he arrives on safe ground, Jack sees Holland driving the *remuda* into the river below the bridge. The horses are swimming bravely across the rough water, although Blue Dart is in trouble, floundering in the current.

Jack rushes down to help Holland who is riding a young bronc with a hackamore that makes it even harder to control. The bronc tries to swim after the other horses, but Holland's weight and the heavy saddle are too much for him and both of them are carried downstream.

Holland kicks his feet from the stirrups, slips over the cantle and down the bronc's hips where he can grasp its tail. A black curly head and a pair of hands tangled in the horse's tail are all that are visible of Holland. The brave little bronc keeps trying but the swift current washes the two of them down the Pecos.

My brother, Holland Bass

When Jack catches up to him on Dogie, he places his boot firmly against Holland's empty saddle and this extra support helps the bronc keep on course. Neck and neck the two horses swim—their manes and Dogie's tail fanned out and floating —Holland truly bringing up the rear.

Finally the two horses manage to get out of the river and clamber up the north bank. Holland turns loose of his pony's tail and grabs the trailing end of the hackamore rope.

Jack takes out his Bull Durham tobacco and they light up.

"I guess my tobacco's halfway to Delaware Crossing by now," Holland says.

Both horses shake vigorously and try to lie down and roll.

Blue Dart, the dapple grey, Papa's favorite mount, is the only one left having trouble with the wild river. The swift current sweeps him over onto his side again and again as he tries to swim after the other horses.

Papa borrows Junior Cass's row boat and he and the boy struggle out into deep water where Blue Dart is drowning.

Papa reaches for the bridle, misses. Blue Dart bares his teeth, ears flat against his head and grabs for the edge of the boat with his teeth.

Once again Papa goes for the bridle and catches it just above the bit. Jerking Blue Dart's head out of the water, he shakes him with all his might.

"Swim, Blue Dart, you old son of a bitch. Swim, God damn you, SWIM!"

I think Blue Dart must have recognized his master's voice because he starts to swim and all the people on the bank cheer wildly. Junior turns the boat toward the north bank.

When he rejoins Holland and Jack, Papa notices that Holland is bareheaded. He takes off his own hat and gives it to Holland.

"Boys, we had a damn close call," he says

Papa is a cusser, but nobody loves horses the way he does.

Now that the danger's over I look to the hills: soft, soft green. The rains have brought the wildflowers out in bunches. In a few days the raging Pecos will grow calm and tame.

CHAPTER SEVEN

THE BASKETBALL GAME

A drink of spring water from the banks of the Pecos around Eddy tastes like a stiff dose of Epsom salts. Nevertheless after a chemical analysis proves that the water is similar in content to the famous springs of Carlsbad, Bohemia, Eddy is no more. Its new name is Carlsbad. Other changes are in the wind.

Five miles west and a little north of Carlsbad, Tawsel Dam is completed and the grass lands bordering the Pecos and in the valley are plowed under. Huge fields of alfalfa and fruit trees replace grama and buffalo grasses.

North of the Pecos is La Huerta, where all the rich people live. Five miles south in Phoenix is a popular gambling place full of drinkers, gamblers and wild women. They say when a gambler has made his pile, he puts his 45 on the table beside his winnings.

Our Uncle Lon Bass operates a Black Jack game there and the first time Holland and Jack go there, Uncle Lon tells them to leave. Then he starts to laugh and says,

"Boys, I mean it—*leave*. If Ed hears about you boys being here he'll not only whip you, he'll whip me, too."

I don't think my brothers left.

Changes and more changes are in the wind. Quite suddenly Papa sells our home at Black River and he trades horses for a house and one hundred sixty acres of land three miles west of Carlsbad. When we move all our friends give us a farewell dance.

Papa leaves the cattle and horses on the open range because there are no fences and the stock drifts from southwest New Mexico to Texas. Stockmen have two roundups a year. During the spring roundup they brand their calves. In the fall they gather the cattle up for sale.

We start to Sunday School in town, but neither Papa nor Mama go with us as they always had at Black River Village. Mama is a little shy, never having lived in town and Papa does not agree with the minister on several issues, especially dancing. For myself, I think the town preaching is entirely too long-winded.

Our school surroundings are also different. On weekday mornings, carrying our lunch in a five-pound lard bucket, we walk to a fine brick schoolhouse with a separate room and teacher for every grade. I feel timid in the town school. My clothes—full skirts that come well below the knee, long sleeves, ruffles at the neck and wrist—look different from the other girls. Town girls wear short sleeves and skirts that just top the knees. I try to explain the difference to Mama, but she won't listen because she thinks I'm being critical of her sewing.

It doesn't take long before I begin to feel very lonely. I miss the closeness of the little school at Black River.

There is one thing that catches my attention: basketball. The game fascinates me. Mama thinks I shouldn't play even though she hasn't seen a game. She says it's rough and "unladylike."

The next school game is against Artesia. Carlsbad's first game. The entire town is excited, but since Mama objects to my playing, I do not ask her to buy me a basketball suit and shoes. Instead, I take up the hem of a four-gored skirt and wear my high-topped laced shoes. Our school colors are blue and white, and my skirt is navy.

We drive to the ball game, Holland, Mama and I, in the buggy. Mama never stops complaining, but Papa overrules her and says I can play.

On the way into town Holland says, "Don't worry, Mama. If anyone makes a remark about her, I'll knock his dad-gummed head off."

Teams and saddle horses are tied near the schoolhouse grounds. Holland finds a place and ties the team. We go through the crowd to my coach and team. They appear not to

34

notice my hemmed up four-gore skirt and hi-top shoes.

Much excitement, the game is on! Artesia has a fine team. Their colors are purple and gold. We are playing neck and neck —meaning the score is even. There is a foul against Artesia and we get a free throw. The coach hands the ball to Camille Grantham, our best goal pitcher. She hands the ball to me and says:

"You make the throw."

I hear my brother's voice booming "I'll bet my whole mount of horse that she makes the goal!"

I do.

A few days after our first game the Chamber of Commerce presents the whole team with suits and shoes. Secretly I wonder if my long dress and hi-top shoes are the reason for this gift.

The girls' basketball team.

16 years old,
Bleach Skull Rank School

CHAPTER EIGHT

THE HORSE RACE

Sister Clara becomes ill suddenly—smallpox, the doctor says. Our family is quarantined. The next thing I know, Clara, who is pregnant with her first child, is dead. It all happens so fast I hardly have a chance to figure any of it out. I see Lyn, her husband, show up one day leading the beautiful horse Handsome Harry back to our house and giving him back to Papa. Clara's wedding band he gives to Mama and then he says goodbye to all of us and leaves New Mexico to start a new life as a law officer in Marenci, Arizona.

This is the low point in the happy days of my youth. Tragedy has struck our family and with one quick blow like lightning, it has claimed a beloved sister and her unborn child. Papa teaches life must be lived in order to be understood and I go on living with a very heavy understanding of what it takes to live and love in this world.

One day some time after Clara's death, a friend of ours, a rancher with a large cattle ranch in the Guadalupe mountains of Queen, spends the night at our house. Ranchers from the east and west side of the Pecos often stay with us when they come to Carlsbad for ranch supplies. My new adventure comes about like this: We are eating breakfast. This friend of our family, Mr. Locklear, turns to me and says,

"I came to Carlsbad to hire a teacher for the Skull Tank School. How would you like to teach for us?"

Papa says, "She's only sixteen."

"Mr. Locklear," I say, speaking up for the first time, "I want to teach and I will do my very best."

Neither Papa nor Mama say another word, but both look at me in surprise.

Then Mr. Locklear tells Papa that I will need a saddle horse. Papa says I can take Handsome Harry. I think immediately of Clara, of her proud wedding, of the fatal bout with smallpox, but I know deep in my heart she would want me to have her beautiful horse on my first job so I accept with gratitude and tears.

The Skull Tank School is ten miles from the little town of Queen, New Mexico. Its location was chosen for its proximity to the only source of water for many miles. The stock-watering tank here is called Skull Tank because of the many cattle skeletons lying all around it.

Mr. Locklear has added a log extension to his ranch house for the Skull Tank teacher to live in. The room is freshly hewn and smells of juniper and pine. They call it Teacher's Room. Sunshine comes in through the cracks in the wall along with the wintery winds when they blow in from the mountains and plains. The room has a bed, a chest of drawers and an organ placed on the north side. I play the organ by ear.

School consists of eight grades and nine pupils, most of them obedient. My problem pupil is a beautiful girl near my own age whose one aim in life is to test my knowledge as a teacher. Each night I study the lessons and work all of the arithmetic problems for the next day's battle with her. Then as fall fades into winter, almost invisibly, my problem pupil loses her hostility and we become good friends.

There are three schools in the mountains, Dark Canyon, Dunaway Seep and Skull Tank. When a dance is announced, all three schools are dismissed at noon.

A fine young gentleman named Holman asks to escort me to the Thanksgiving dance. He rides up on a sorrel roan named Roanie, saddles Handsome Harry for me, ties my ball dress in a flour sack behind my saddle.

I have baked a three layer cowbell's cake the night before and I put it on a dinner plate which I then put into a flour sack and all this is balanced on top of my saddlehorn.

Flour sacks are in great demand, not only for dress and cake carriers, but also for drawers.

One of the cowboys gathered outside the dance shouts as we ride up:

"Holman, I'll bet you the teacher's horse can beat Old Roanie in a pacing race."

Holman straightens up in his saddle and seems to notice Harry for the first time.

"Not a horse on the mountaintop can stay in Roanie's dust," he says. "Shor, I'll bet you."

I ease Harry toward him, intending to tell him Harry's a racer and a thoroughbred, but Harry reads my mind, tosses his head, champs the bit and arches his neck.

Harry is begging me to race.

One of the boys steps to the ground and with his boot heel marks a line across the mountain road. I hand my cake to another boy and come up to the starting line.

Someone fires a six shooter and at the sound of the shot I tighten the reins and lean slightly forward. Harry and Roanie take off nose to nose.

In a moment, Harry leaves Roanie far behind.

After the race the boys rawhide (tease) Holman unmercifully and poor Holman dances only the first and last dances with me. The rest of the time he mopes outside.

I won the race. But I lost my beau.

CHAPTER NINE

STRANGERS

The ranchers in the Guadalupe Mountains burn oak and juniper wood. Pine is the most difficult to get out of the rough mountains and it is used only for kindling. The moment I smell the fragrant odor of burning juniper I go right back to my childhood on the plains and those evenings sitting around the cookstove with the tent flaps tied back and the call of a plover out there in the windy prairie.

Mr. Locklear's house, like most ranch houses, has a dugout with a fireplace. A dugout is a family room with a fireplace, chairs and bed; some dugouts also have cookstoves and dining tables.

One late afternoon when the Locklear children and I ride home from school, we notice a tent stretched near the teacher's room. This tent is furnished with a bed only.

We notice several horses saddled and tied to the hitching rack. The doctor's horse is among them—a black branded F.

Earlier that day Mr. Locklear had saddled his horse Trannie and had ridden out among his cattle to find, settled in a lonely canyon, a covered wagon. Nearby, a man was cooking over a campfire and his two children were playing next to him.

Mr. Locklear rode up to the man and stepping down from Trannie and dropping his bridle reins, he said:

"Howdy, stranger. Aren't you new on the mountain top?"

"I hope you don't mind our camping on your range," the man said. "I needed a camp near water. My wife is sick. Been sick for over a year. The doctor advised me to come west with her. He said the high dry air would heal her lungs. We followed the stock and found this spring."

Mr. Locklear walked to the wagon and put his head inside.

The lady, Mrs. Johnson, lay back in the wagon. Mr. Johnson had propped her up with a lot of pillows. She was very pale and her voice was low and weak. There was an unnatural, bright color in her cheeks. With her black hair and large blue eyes, Mrs. Johnson was a beautiful lady.

However, Mr. Locklear realized she was dangerously ill.

"Load the wagon and the children. I'll get the team and hitch up," he said when he got back to the fire.

Mr. Johnson was ladling breakfast onto some tin plates. He looked startled.

"I'm not a claim jumper. Are you putting me off your land?" His Winchester leaned against a nearby tree; he walked over to it and said, "I have a very sick wife."

Mr. Locklear, laughing, answered:

"Hold your fire, friend, I'm taking you people to my home. We can take care of your wife better there than you can here. Now let's get going."

That afternoon they hurriedly move my things out of the teacher's room and put Mrs. Johnson in my bed. I'm to stay in a tent, I have a bed with my suitcase underneath, a little stand in the corner for my comb and brush.

Mr. Locklear changes saddle horses and rides a fine saddle-gaited horse to Queen to fetch the doctor.

Late in the night I am awakened by a noise. I sit up in bed. The moonlight is very bright shining through the white tent walls so I can clearly make out the doctor, undressed, climbing into bed with me.

I jump up and grab my clothes and start for the front of the tent. The doctor growls in exhaustion.

"What the hell are you doing sleeping in this tent?"

Then he grabs his clothes and charges for the entrance, running into the center pole on the way out and collapsing the tent on both of us. We are on our knees, bumping heads, struggling to find an opening.

When the doctor and I crawl forth, my long-sleeved nightgown trails in the dust. He is crawling around in a pair of long underwear, muttering to himself and dragging his clothes while an assembled audience from the house is roaring at the spectacle we are both making.

"Somebody find my britches," the doctor bellows.

Mr. Locklear, laughing with the best of them, takes me by the arm.

"Go on to the dugout and sleep with my wife. Doctor and I will sleep in his camp bed.

Five days pass and although the doctor gives Mrs. Johnson the best care he can and everyone prays for her speedy recovery, she just gets worse and worse, and one day when the doctor goes into her room to check on her she is found sleeping peacefully, out of harm, finally free of suffering. The cowboys from all around pass the hat for Mrs. Johnson's funeral. With this money, Mr. Johnson can afford a proper burial and with what is left over, he will be able to return to Texas with his two children.

So many lives come and go as I am growing that I begin to understand: life is nothing but a coming and a going. We are born and we die, it's what's in the middle we don't know much about until after it has happened. But then maybe death is that way too.

I don't know.

CHAPTER TEN

MOUNTAIN CATTLE CROSSING

The north wind is whistling among the oak and juniper trees, yellow and crimson leaves fall about the campfire. Daylight is breaking and the men hear the camp cook, Wild Horse, giving his call:

"Come and get it, or out she goes."

The cowboys, Toughie in the lead, go to the chuck box. Each man fills his tin plate with a light and fluffy sourdough biscuit, hot tender steak, lick (syrup) and Arbuckle coffee, hot and strong.

Wild Horse is a fine chuck wagon cook and a top cow hand.

Toughie is the horse wrangler. Right after breakfast, he saddles a little black baldfaced horse called Rabbit who downs his head and starts to buck. Toughie see-saws the bits and finally pulls Rabbit's head up. Toughie is not really what you call a bronc buster, but he knows how to stay on top when he needs to. Now, he hurries off among the trees to bring the saddle horses for all the cowboys.

Joe and Salty finish their breakfast, scrape out their plates and set plates and cups in the chuck wagon lid; this is a ritual, an unwritten law. Like Toughie, they are hurrying to relieve the night guards around the herd of cattle.

Night guards often sing softly when riding the night herd and it is beautiful and mournful to hear them sing.

Breakfast is over. Toughie arrives with the saddle horses. The men are just finishing a rope corral, made by tying their saddle ropes to trees. John Smith holds one end of the rope and ties it to a tree after the last horse trots into the pen.

Wild Horse hitches up the team and drives off over the rugged mountain trail, bed rolls piled high on the wagon top.

Dolph Shattuck says, "Fellers, we'll make Mosely Springs tonight."

Johnnie-behind-the-Deuce (so-called because of his prowess in a poker game) saddles Tumbleweed. He eases into the saddle, Tumbleweed quits the earth and paws at the pine cones high in the trees. He stands on his head, almost. Johnnie-behind-the-Deuce is a bronco buster, but he also knows the cattle drive to Mosely is hard and long and he stays aboard Tumbleweed holding a tight rein and keeping him moving in a slow lope up toward the herd.

Then the rest of the men mount and ride out to the cattle, allowing them to scatter and graze on the mountains, pointed east toward Carlsbad seventy miles away. Slowly, yet under control, the cattle drift over the mountains like brown and white clouds.

Early in the afternoon, Wild Horse pulls up at Mosely Springs, unhitches and hobbles the wagon team.

After Mosely, the next permanent watering place is Sitting Bull Falls, some twenty miles northeast. Sitting Bull, whose Indian name was Tatanka Yotanka, was the Teton Sioux Chief who fought against Custer at Little Big Horn. Mosely Springs has seen many a desperate battle between Indian and white man and it has also been a hideout for cattle rustlers in the early days.

Wild Horse builds a fire and sets the sourdough biscuits on some stones to rise. He knows the herd will not arrive before sundown so he strips and bathes in the creek. Then he decides to wash his clothes, scrubbing them on a large flat rock with a bar of lye soap, happily singing *Buffalo Girls* loud and clear as he hangs his shirt and pants on the bushes to dry.

Wearing only a pair of boots, Wild Horse starts the supper. Suddenly, down the steep mountain trail, he hears the sound of shod horses, looks up and sees two riders. One of them is a woman! The only garment he hasn't washed is his slicker, which he hastily puts on. The slicker reaches below his knees in front, but is open in the back — "vented" as the style magazines would say — from the hips down.

Andy Black approaches, escorting the schoolmarm from the Hess ranch. It is Saturday. They've come to meet the cattle drive and eat supper. Black spies Wild Horse's wet clothes hanging on the bushes and his face lights up with pleasure.

Helping the teacher from her side-saddle, Andy seats her upon a big rock. His polished boots shine like new money. *He polished them for the teacher's benefit*, Wild Horse is thinking. Grimly he clutches the slicker together in front, looks down at his hairy legs and the knobby knees above his boot tops.

"Hey, Wild Horse, how about a cup of Java?" Andy says.

There's a dev'lish look in his eyes. This is not the first time he and Wild Horse have locked horns.

"Help yourselves," Wild Horse answers.

"Wild Horse, you know I don't know where you keep your stuff. And you know I wouldn't want to go snooping in your drawers."

Wild Horse is rightly named, but when his fur is rubbed the wrong way, he's more like a mountain boar hog than a stallion. His 30-30 leans against an old oak tree and is not too far away. Gingerly, he sidesteps toward it, clutching the slicker with his left hand while he picks up the Winchester and throws a cartridge into the barrel with his right — and now the dev'lish look is in *his* deep blue eyes.

"Andy," he drawls, "yore boots shine like new money and I bet the cost of them set you back a month's pay."

Wild Horse aims the gun at Andy's right foot.

"I'm bettin' you five dollars I can clip yore boot heel off and never touch yore foot. Put up yore five dollars. I'm bettin' I can do just that."

The teacher rises, looking horrified.

Andy stoops down beside her. She places her foot in his hand and he tosses her into her saddle. Then Andy mounts, turns and both horses go down the trail leading back over the mountains.

The teacher says, not quite out of earshot, "Andy, I don't think that cowboy had on any under-lings beneath that slicker."

Andy doesn't say a word.

CHAPTER ELEVEN

THE CARLSBAD ANGEL

The cowboys and their herd finally arrive at West Canal Bridge, three miles west of Carlsbad with a bunch of mountain cattle that have never crossed any kind of bridge before. They refuse to step on the rough timber of the bridge. Again and again the cowboys push them to the edge where they get panicky. the cows bawl, the big steers break from the herd and run and, for a while, it looks like there might be a stampede.

Dolph, riding Opal, is wet with sweat and caked with dust. John Cantreel is riding a big brown horse, Go Devil. He's an old trail boss and cow puncher and now he rides up to Dolph, pulling out his Bull Durham tobacco and rolling himself a *cigareete.*

"Dolph," he says, "they'll never do'er."

"Well, John, I'm kinda like these mountain cattle myself, not downright accustomed to lumber bridges. This is your territory, so why don't you take over."

John turns the herd south and drives them through San Jose, a small Mexican village south of Carlsbad. He pays a man to let them go through his land and solves the whole problem.

Before sundown they have the mountain cattle corralled and the drive is over.

John and most of the boys change horses and gallop into Carlsbad and round themselves up a game of stud poker.

Dolph and the others roll out their bedrolls near the shipping pens. Dolph has signed a contract for the entire herd and he doesn't intend to let the herd out of his sight until he receives the money for it. The campfire burns low. Dolph searches in his pocket for the list that Susie, his wife, gave him before he left home early in the morning.

By the dim firelight Dolph reads: *Dear Dolphie. Choose a dress (black), a new Bible for your mother and a Sunday shirt for you. Love, Susie.*

Why, I'll buy her the prettiest dress in town, pink, trimmed with white lace.
Susie is a beautiful lady — another one of my sisters.

After supper, two cowboys ride out to stand night guard over the cattle, the sun sinking behind the mountains in the west. Dave Williams starts for the chuck wagon to get his bedroll.
"Look, fellers," he says. "Looky yonder!"
A great black cloud is rising into the sky from the ground.
They stand in awe as the cloud drifts over their heads. Then they see that what appears to be a cloud is actually thousands and thousands of bats.
One of the cowboys finds a huge hole in the ground — it's the bat cave, the now-world famous Carlsbad Caverns — which they have to abandon investigating because it's growing dark.
Early next morning, they return to the hole and tie some saddle ropes together.
John Angel volunteers to be let down into it.
They make a large loop in the rope, for John to sit in as in a swing. Gently, the men play out the rope — but suddenly it starts to twist in their hands and they hear John holler bloody murder.
When they pull him out, John loosens himself from the rope and steps away from the hole in the ground and takes a deep breath.
"What'd you see, John?"
"Gimme a smoke, fellers. You ain't going to believe me."
"Believe what?" asks Rusty Jones.
"I saw a beautiful mansion made of polished rock. Stately pillars reaching high. A room one hundred feet deep. Water glistening at the bottom. Air fresh as heaven..."

CHAPTER TWELVE

KNOWLES

Knowles, New Mexico, is located in the center of Mr. Knowles' horse range. For years, Mr. Knowles has operated a tiny store and post office in his home. Now Knowles is in the center of what appears to be a real boom town. Men with their teams hitched to scrapers, fresnoes and plows are clearing a roadway for a railroad which will connect Knowles with Midland, Texas, ninety miles east, and on the northwest with Roswell which is about the same distance.

A very nice schoolhouse and a bank building have just been erected.

Knowles' rival, Lovington, New Mexico, is about twenty miles north and these two little sister villages are like two dandy quarter horses in a race, each vying with the other for the inside track.

I now have a first grade certificate and I apply for a position in the Knowles Graded School. They accept me.

Very early in the morning I board the mail car. Knowles is eighty miles from Carlsbad along a hazardous road and as we pass through the James' range (the James brothers are ranchers of Eddy County), the mail driver stops at a mail box and asks a man standing nearby:

"How's the road ahead?"

'That road ahead is pretty tough titty," he fires back and my face starts to burn. "If you have trouble," he continues, "just blow your car whistle and I'll be there with my team in thirty minutes. These stud horses of mine can pull a freight train across the sand hills."

Again, I am blushing. Mama never allowed the word *stud* to be used at home, *stallion* being the more refined word.

But soon we glide swiftly over the road and at about three in the afternoon we arrive safely. Many people have come to meet the mail car: men with big hats and high-heeled boots; ladies wearing pretty ruffled bonnets of red, green, blue and yellow. They look like wild flowers on the prairie.

I'm a little frightened, a perfect stranger with no place to board and room.

Then a tall handsome man walks up to the mail car and, smiling, tips his hat to me.

"You're the little Bass girl, aren't you?"

I nod.

He says, "Holland's a good friend of mine; we made the JAL roundup together last fall."

So he takes me to his home and on the way explains that I am to be their guest until a place can be arranged for me to board and room.

The house is stately — a white two-story building. As we drive up I remember the teacher's room at Queen with those unchinked logs and the tent I slept in when Mrs. Johnson was ill. This fine home stands in strong contrast to those humble surroundings. The people, though, are just the same — grand and noble.

Mrs. Heard meets us at the door. She is a beautiful and gracious lady, the former Mabel Grey, daughter of Tom Grey, a prominent cattle rancher. The large Grey ranch is south of Carlsbad in the Mosely Springs area.

Fall glides into winter, the cold blizzards blow, the cattle drift with the wintry winds. There are no drift fences here and the cowmen, tough and rugged as the land itself, keep an eye on their brands.

The poor sheep herders mostly herd their bands of sheep on foot. Sometimes they freeze to death.

CHAPTER THIRTEEN

THE DANCE OVER THE BANK

Spring, Leap Year, 1912.

The ladies are planning a Leap Year dance to be held in the bank building, a two-story edifice with the entire upper story used exclusively for a dance hall. The ladies get to choose their escorts.

The invitation reads like this:

You are invited to a Cowboy Ball
To be given Feb. 10th at the new dance hall.
Our country is undergoing a great change
This will be the last roundup on the High Lonesome range.
Let's round up our stock and get ready to go
We got to get ready for the man with the hoe.
No more chuck wagons, we'll eat at the shack
And turn our cow ponies into a Kaffir corn stack.
We'll throw them together on the hill
Just east of Old Eleven Wind Mill,
Not very far from the edge of the sands
Where the town of Knowles now stands.
Bill O'Neal the pool wagon Boss
Will meet you at the gate and make you come across.
Bill Franklin will lead us on the drive
As soon as all the stray men arrive.
Jack Heard will have the tally book
And see that all the stray men get a look.
The nearest water will be the Cap Rock
Be sure to come and get your stock.

I have my eye on Pat Thorn from Thornville, a handsome fellow, but not too good a dancer. I tell my friend, Estelle

Mauldin that I'm planning to ask Pat and she doesn't say a word. You see, Estelle is teaching in Thornville, a little school five miles north of Knowles and she has already asked Pat to be *her* escort! Mail is pretty slow so Pat, who receives my invitation too late, rides into Knowles to explain he's already Estelle's escort.

Now I have less than a week but as luck would have it, I manage to find a cowboy who will take me to the big *baile*.

A couple of days before the dance two young men, Bunk Ship and Floyd Dawson, ask Miss Mamie Lyons and me to go horseback riding. Since Mamie is spending the weekend with me, we accept and Bunk leads his beautiful black race horse for Mamie to ride while Floyd leads a grey TX horse for me.

The boys hold the horses for us as we mount and then we are off in a high lope.

This little TX horse starts to run. I can't stop him. The boys holler, "Stop him, Eva!" I'm *trying* to stop him, but he's gone cold-jaw — clamped the bits between his teeth. I see-saw the reins, trying to loosen them with no luck.

A cold windy afternoon and a TX horse that really wants to run, and suddenly looming ahead is a four-strand barbed wire fence.

The grey TX horse hits that barbed wire fence like a locomotive and turns a complete somersault over it. I'm thrown clear of the fence and the horse, but when I sit up my shoulder is out of the socket.

Dr. Schaffer comes along in his buggy — one of the boys rode off to get him — and puts my shoulder back in place and hangs my arm in a sling.

When school is over on the Day of Days, a package arrives for me and I eagerly open it.

It's a beautiful dress from Mama! Cream beige with a deep flounce on the skirt, a bertha around the shoulders and a wide crushed belt, all in blue satin.

I take the bandage off my shoulder and pour one half of my cologne into the wash tub full of water. There is no fire in my room and February is a cold month on the plains, but nothing is going to interfere with my bath.

After bathing, I light the coal oil lamp and heat my curling iron. My left arm is useless, but the hand works fine. The hardest part is getting my corset laced right. I look over at my beautiful slim-waisted dress and lace the corset as tight as I can stand it.

I look into my looking glass with my new dress on and see last summer's hat hanging nearby on the wall. It has a wreath of red roses around the brim. I tear two petals from one of those last-summer roses, douse the petals with cologne and daintily tint my cheeks and lips. I take one last look in the mirror and think, *Art can beat Nature any time.* My dress is shoe-top length, I wear black pumps.

Jim drives up in a new buggy. I don't know where he borrowed it and I think it cost him money and persuasive talk to obtain this buggy for tonight, just for me and my lame shoulder.

People come from the Brakes, the Cap Rock, Carlsbad and for miles around Knowles. Horses are tied to the hitching rails all over town, the lone barber shop is overflowing with dusty cowboys.

We climb the stairs; they are already dancing. Jim takes a red silk handkerchief from his pocket. It is large and beautiful. He folds it once over his right hand and says,

"Shall we dance?"

We are off to the tune of *Over the Waves.* In an effort to protect my arm and shoulder Jim gives my new pumps a bad time.

I laugh and tell him not to let my bad arm interfere with a beautiful waltz. Gracefully we glide in and out of the throngs of dancers. Jim proves to be a good dancer after all, and just as we're finishing a waltz, someone touches me on my good arm and says, "Howdy."

I look up into the blue, blue eyes of Tom Pendleton. A beautiful girl is with him.

53

The next dance is a polka, the *Highland Fling* and Tom comes over and asks me to dance with him.

Shyly I nod yes. I am shy because this particular polka brings to mind a twilight concert long ago when I awkwardly tripped and fell flat on my face.

We finish the polka. Toms walks me to my seat, holding my hand and leans very close to me. I can feel his breath on my cheek and I start to blush.

He whispers very low in my ear, "I'll stay over 'til Sunday if you'll give me a date."

"Please stay over," is all I can manage to say.

"By the way, what happened to your arm?"

I tell him of the grey TX horse.

"I broke that horse, worthless cold jaw that he is. What fool put you on him?"

I put a finger to my lips and motion toward my friend dancing next to us.

CHAPTER FOURTEEN

THE BANK ROBBERY

Few people are on the streets because of the sand storm. Most of the men are in the saloon playing cards, Knowles being the only town east of the Pecos that has a saloon.

A cowboy rides into Knowles, heads straight for the saloon.

"The Seminole Bank's been robbed," he says matter of factly. Quietly the card players lay down their cards, their faces blank. Then several speak at once: "When? Who? Did they get the money?"

The bartender offers whiskey and the cowboy nods.

Sipping his drink, he tells them:

"Two strangers ride into Seminole this morning. They're riding two of Uncle Joe Graham's saddle horses, a bay and a brown. Front street's deserted, the manager's alone in the bank. The two strangers walk up to the banker, draw and cock their six-shooters and say, 'Hand over the cash.' Each of them is carrying a meal sack. First they stuff the greenbacks into the sacks and they they stuff the sacks into their shirts. After that they mount Uncle Joe's saddle horses and vanish into the sand storm."

Texas and New Mexico sheriffs, along with Uncle Joe and his son Jodie, search all over the red sand hills, but no tracks are left because the sand storm has swept them away.

The postmaster at Pearl tells the sheriffs that a couple of days before the robbery two strangers came in on a mail car, each one carrying a saddle, and they asked for directions to some rancher's home. They left Pearl walking, carrying their saddles on their shoulders.

The rancher is located and questioned. He and his wife were at Monument, sixty miles west of Seminole, the day the bank

55

was being robbed. The rancher has no enemies, he is loved by everyone.

Then Uncle Joe Graham's horses are found loose on the range showing signs of hard and fast riding.

Still the robbers have left no trail.

Months pass and the cowpunchers are making their fall round-up branding the late calves and gathering cattle to ship to market when they discover the skeleton of a man in what appears to have been a camp hidden in the sands.

One of the bank robbers must have murdered his friend for the loot and then disappeared with the March wind across the desert. What happened to him, whether he made it to safety with all the money in the Seminole Bank, remains a mystery. But the skeleton of the dead man is positively identified by dental work done in Oklahoma.

The rest is the secret of the wind.

CHAPTER FIFTEEN

THE SPOONERS' RIG

I board the mail car once more, this time for home.

The mail driver encounters no trouble and we arrive in Carlsbad near four o'clock. My folks live three miles west of Carlsbad, but I have a close friend who lives right in town, Lillie Scott. The mail driver takes me to her home.

Her handsome brother, Louis, has just that day returned from the TX roundup and he goes to the livery stable to get a horse and buggy to take me home.

When he returns from the stable driving a well-known horse named Slitz and a fancy buggy with fringe on top, I have to smile. This horse and buggy are much sought after by all the young men and they're known as the *Spooners' Rig*.

Louis comes in to bathe and change clothes, he smiles and winks at me. Lillie suggests she and I take a little ride while Louis is occupied.

Over at the City Livery Barn, we meet Tom Pendleton who is the owner of the stable. When Tom sees us, he motions Lillie to stop, he climbs in, laughing, and takes the reins. Then he drives us back to the Scott home.

Louis is still in the bathroom. My suitcase is sitting on the floor near the door.

"Louis," Tom calls through the door, "there'll be no charge for Slitz and the buggy."

He takes me by the arm with one hand, and with the other he grabs my suitcase and we go out to the Spooners' Rig.

Suddenly all my good raising says to wait for Louis, but my heart says to go with Tom. Briefly I am caught between the two hovering like a hummingbird. Then I make my decision and climb into the buggy with Tom.

Tom Pendleton, 22 years old

We drive over the old canal bridge, the water rippling and swift. I explain to Tom that I'll be teaching at Rocky come fall. This is the best paid country school in Eddy County and is only twenty miles from Carlsbad.

Tom takes my hand. "I have a contract I'd like to discuss with you. . ." he says. But just then we drive up to our gate and Papa and Mama rush out to the buggy.

Tom nods politely to them and although they ask him to stay for supper, he thanks them and leaves.

Papa, Mama and I walk out to the corrals where the sheep are huddled close and Handsome Harry neighs in my direction, telling me Howdy. He is an old horse now, but just as beautiful and high stepping as ever.

Early the next morning, right after breakfast, Tom rides up to the kitchen door. Papa sees him coming and says, "That cowpuncher sure doesn't let the grass grow under his feet."

Tom is leading a fine-looking black horse. When I go out, he hands the rope to me and dismounts.

"Tom, what a beautiful horse!"

"Midnight is a down payment on that contract that I mentioned yesterday."

Then he saddles Midnight while I rush inside to change into my riding clothes.

I had ridden Blue-eyed Johnnie, a quarter horse, and Handsome Harry, a pacer, in races — much to my mother's disgust. Mama commented one day after a horse race, "I never thought I'd see the day when one of my daughters entered a horse race."

But I didn't agree with Mama and her southern-lady standards and I failed to see anything wrong with a good horse race — especially if you rode the winner — and both those horses were winners.

Now I take Midnight on a race all our own, across the grassy flats. Tom follows on his horse and we stop under an old Hackberry tree. Blackbirds and cooing doves burst from the branches as we pull up to rest.

Tom walks up to Midnight's side to help me dismount. As I

slip to the ground I find myself in Tom's arms. We sit on a fallen log beneath the Hackberry tree.

Tom says, "The contract I referred to is for life. I love you, Eva."

My heart is singing and my face is blushing. Tom leans over and kisses me on the lips.

"Do you love me?" he asks.

"Yes, Tom."

I'm so happy I want to say, "Let's get married today." But a girl must be modest and ladylike and ought to keep her feelings laced up inside.

Wild flowers are blooming on the prairie, morning glories hang from the limb of the old tree. Tom reaches up and plucks a trailing vine. Then he breaks off a stem of Indian Paint Brush and gives me both in a bouquet.

I know I will remember this day, the blackbirds and the doves, the gentle direct way Tom asks me to be his wife, and the casual way he hands me his rough-made prairie bouquet, for as long as the grass grows in the plains and the wild horses shake their heads in the sun.

PART TWO

CHAPTER SIXTEEN

HOME ON THE PLAINS

Daylight is breaking on the plains; I hear the low howling of coyotes and the milk cows lowing to their calves. Tom and I are sitting at the kitchen table drinking coffee, finishing our second cup while our little daughter, Hazel Marie, sleeps in the adjoining room. Tom picks up the milk buckets and we start to the corral to milk the cows.

I look back at our home. It is beautiful in the soft light of the new day. Morning glory vines cover the front porch with full blooms of red, blue and white. The wheel of the windmill gently turns, clear sparkling water falls into the large square stock tank. Old and huge cottonwood trees grow along the banks and tiny goldfish swim and make love in the clear water. We love our tiny home on the prairie, but along with many others just like us, we face some serious difficulties.

All of the free range is being fenced, we are badly over-stocked and Tom is trying to sell our stock horses. Automobiles are putting horsemen out of business and, as a result, two good saddle horses today can do what it used to take a remuda of ten head of horses to do in the past.

There are no more round-ups. The model-T Ford with its short skirts or high fenders, is the most popular make of car on a country road. We discuss the free open range that still exists in the southwestern part of New Mexico, Tom and I, again and again at the breakfast table. It beckons to us. So much wind has blown over the plains since we got married and moved to our first home in Monument, New Mexico.

In the weeks that pass, Tom negotiates the sale of our ranch and cattle to Skillet Houston, a neighbor of ours who has a ranch a few miles northwest of us.

Skillet's real name is Harry.

Let me tell you how he acquired the name Skillet:

One night a bunch of cow-punchers were sitting around a campfire. Somehow they decided to vote on the ugliest fellow in camp. Harry, actually, is a handsome cowboy who stands over six feet, with brown eyes, black curly hair and always smiling. But he received all the votes. Wild Horse Hill picked up the old skillet that lay near the camp fire. "And here's yore beauty prize," he said, extending the skillet to Skillet.

Anyway, Tom and I are asked to host a Christmas dance for Skillet who is a bachelor. People come from all directions, some in cars, a few families in wagons, but most of the guests still ride horseback. At midnight, the men build a fire beneath a big iron wash kettle which they fill with water and pour in several pounds of Arbuckle coffee. It starts to boil and Tom stirs it with a branding iron and pours in another gallon of cold water to settle it.

In the picture shows they make you think cowboys are always drunk. — Well, maybe they do take a drink or two and once in a while a cowboy hits the bottle too often and too hard and then the other cowboys have to put him to bed.

One time at a dance in Monument one of the cowboys had too much *red-eye* and his friend told him, "Jim, you're drunk. Go outside."

"I know it," Jim said. "I'm just waiting for that door to come around again so I can go through it."

Skillet's big Christmas dance is our last one in that part of New Mexico.

It is March. Time once more to load the wagon. Tom has a large canopy made for it because we plan to sleep in it on our trek west.

Our wild stock horses are quite difficult to drive the first few days. This is especially true of the mares in foal. They are just like salmon — they want to go back to their spawning grounds and have their colts on their own home range.

The second night we arrive at the P.E.N. Ranch, Tom's boyhood home and one of the cowboys who has come in from Carlsbad tells us all about Pancho Villa's raid. Villa crossed the border into the states at Columbus, New Mexico.

One of Tom's friends says, "Tom, Columbus isn't far from where you're headed. I think you're making a big mistake."

However, Tom and I are cattle people and we're banking heavily on free range — range that has a carrying capacity of thirty-five head to the section — and not even Pancho Villa is going to stop us.

Very early the next morning we hitch Paul and Syntax, our wheelers, to the wagon. Good and Atkins are our leaders. At Lone Tree a boy in his teens asks to join us. He wants to leave the Pecos River country and we're glad to have him.

The third day we arrive at the tiny village of Queen. This is beautiful land and fine stock country but it has one drawback: lack of water.

Two cowboys, Chuck and Charlie, ask Tom if they may go along with us. We pass through El Paso Gap. The people there have just been granted a post office service. Mr. Thomas is the first postmaster of El Paso Gap.

The west winds blow almost daily. I find myself repeating these lines, only I change the wording:

Blow, blow, ye sandy winds; your sands cut
no deeper than my longing for my loved ones
and the dear home that we have left behind on the plains.

I think the original is:

Blow, Blow, ye wintry winds. Ye cut no deeper
than remorse.

from the *Bible*

Tom is always cheerful, I do not mention to him I am home-sick. In passing through Salt Flats we are forced to make long drives. Water for our horses is scarce. So is wood. We have a

65

five gallon keg attached to the side of the wagon and a tin cup on a small chain fastened to the water keg for a dipper.

The men do most of the cooking. Sometimes there is no wood, so we cook with cow chips.

The first thing I do when we stop the wagon for the day is open the chuck wagon. Its lid serves as a camp table for preparing all of our meals. Then I make the sourdough biscuits and set them aside to rise. Cow chips produce heat quickly, but they burn to ash just as quickly. The boys pile them high on the Dutch oven lid and set the Dutch oven over the red coals.

Later — much later — we are traveling in the Cox range east of Las Cruces. Tom asks Mr. Cox for permission to lay over for a few days and Mr. Cox tells us to make ourselves right at home. When we're ready to leave, Tom offers Mr. Cox a beautiful yearling colt, one of the stallion Prince's colts, but Mr. Cox refuses by saying, "No, thank you. I am horse poor."

This is Mr. Cox's gracious way of saying that he wouldn't think of charging for the grass and water.

We name the pony Little Prince. After he's been broken, Tom makes a present of him to me — what a fine horse! Little Prince never waltzes around a mesquite bush or a sacahuista, he always jumps them. Sometimes I have to really claw leather to stay aboard Little Prince.

We come to Ora Grande, a very small town and the boys lope to the store to buy an El Paso paper. We read of the gruesome war Pancho Villa's waging south of the border, very close to where we plan to make our new home. We also gain our first knowledge of the I.W.W. strike by the Industrial Workers of the World, sometimes known as "I Won't Work." The mine owners are badly in need of workers, and the wage is over eight dollars per day.

Chuck and Charlie tell us they want to go to Bisbee to work in the mines. They flag the train at Ora Grande and wave their sombreros back at us. We wave adios to them. They are good boys, we'll miss them.

Again I drive the wagon with Hazel Marie on the wagon seat

beside me. At Organ Gap, now called Organ Pass, the road is narrow and rough and Tom drives the horses south of Las Cruces and swims them across the Rio Grande.

From the wagon seat I view Las Cruces for the first time. The trees are soft green, the fruit trees are in full blossom. Every house has its own emerald-green yard.

But my rapture over the view turns to fear when I see a car coming toward me. Custom declares the horse and wagon to leave the road for an oncoming car. I look at the narrow rugged road before me with its large boulders so close to the edge and, as the Model T throttles down into low gear, I decide come hell or high water I'm not moving over.

The driver of the Model T turns out of the road dodging bushes and boulders and he shouts "Howdy!" as he passes, tipping his hat.

My silk bonnet is on the wagon seat. I pick it up and wave it back gratefully in his direction.

Then Tom rides up. "Are you O.K.? You look awfully pale."

"Tom, I met a car."

"Were the horses frightened?"

"Not a bit. I was the one who was scared."

We both laugh.

Now it's the wagon's turn to cross the Rio Grande, running full and no bridge. Tom stops the team and brakes it.

A man, sitting under a beautiful cottonwood tree by the river, tosses his cigarette into the river, comes over to the wagon and says confidently, "I'll drive your team across the river for fifty cents."

"What for?" Tom says.

"I know this here river," the man says.

"And I know my team."

Tom tightens the lines on the lead team, releases the wagon brake and hollers, "Let's go, boys!"

Daintily, the leaders step into the Rio Grande, the water comes over the hub caps of the wheels. He crosses the Rio Grande for the first time in our wagon without a hitch.

The cigarette-smoking stranger on the opposite bank goes back to the cottonwood to daydream some more.

Still the west winds blow. We continue west. The grass turf is thin everywhere we look. Our stock horses which were wild when we left home are now tame. They follow behind the wagon like pets, but this is no country for a horse ranch.

Two more days and we are in Hachita County. Hachita is a small village on the Southern Pacific Railway and ranchers come from as far as seventy-five miles to buy all of their supplies on credit from the Hachita Mercantile Store. Once a year, after cattle sales, they pay back what they owe. Sometimes after severe droughts when there are no cattle sales, there's no money either, but we hear that the owner of the store, Mr. Frank Brown, never cuts anyone off when he is trying to make good.

From Hachita we turn south and then west where the range is wonderful with blue and black grama grass and some buffalo grass. The ground has a turf of grass, weed and brush to browse. Apache Plume grows on the banks of the arroyos and the Indian Paint Brush is in full bloom.

Our stock horses scatter and graze in the soft green grass. The Sierra Madre Mountains are tree-covered soft lavender, rising majestically to the south of us just across the border in Mexico. On our right is Animas Mountain. Javelina hogs and domestic hogs that have become wild roam these mountains and make good hunting.

Tom rides up to the side of the wagon, takes off his hat and points to the sloping hills and valleys directly before us.

"A rancher's paradise," he exclaims.

In a few days he rides the seventy-five miles back to Hachita and takes the train there for El Paso to buy some cattle. After making his purchase, he ships the cattle to Hachita, unloads them and, on the second day of the trail drive, late in the afternoon Tom stops at a lake to let the cattle drink.

Tom takes his hat off, scoops up water in the brim and is drinking when a rider appears and says gruffly, "I'm John

Parks, Cattle Inspector. Show me your bill of sale for these cattle."

"I bought them from a Mr. Ammett in El Paso," Tom says, "but I do not have my bill of sale with me."

"Then, I demand that you turn the cattle loose until you produce a bill of sale for them."

Tom's papers are in Hachita along with his dirty clothes, so he turns Loma Gray back the way they came and arrives sometime after nightfall in Hachita.

That night there is a heavy rainfall and the cattle scatter for miles. In order to get them all back, Tom (after showing Parks the bill of sale) has to do a special fall roundup.

Tom knows the chairman of the New Mexico Sanitary Board and he relates the circumstances to him. Mr. Parks gets fired but this doesn't help Tom.

The Victoria Land and Cattle Company, known locally as the Diamond-A's, own almost all of the deeded land in this part of New Mexico. They are called "The Diamond A Outfit." The owners, William Randolph Hearst and others, live in far away cities, but their general manager, Walter Birchfield, lives in Deming, New Mexico. All of the deputy sheriffs and cattle inspectors are furnished free room and board by The Diamond A Outfit. They hire many people and furnish houses for all of their employees. Thousands of horses and cattle roam this rich country, most of them carrying The Diamond A Outfit's brand.

The influence of The Diamond A Outfit is considerable and the independent rancher, like Tom, is in a tough place during a tough time.

Our County Seat is Silver City, a hundred fifty miles west. There, the feuds are settled with six guns. Very few women live in this rough border country, and we're expecting our second baby.

After making a sale on our cattle, Tom signs a contract with the Arizona Gypsum and Plaster Company to haul and deliver gypsum and we must be on the move again. The road to Douglas through the Guadalupe Mountains — narrow and rugged, lined with boulders — is dangerous.

We have four horses hitched to our heavily loaded wagon. Black-Man, a fine and trusty horse, is the wheeler on the right. We are traveling down a very steep incline and Tom has the wagon brake on and is holding the lines tightly. Black-man, the right wheeler, is saddled. Tom slips from wagon to saddle and gently talks to Black-Man when the road is steep and dangerous. He stops the team and climbs back on the wagon seat to rest them for a moment.

There is a bad piece of road up ahead and we start down it with great trepidation. Suddenly, the loaded wagon rolls almost on top of the wheelers. The brake is gone, burning so hot it has given way. Tom talks to the team and tries to hold them back. Black-Man slides to his haunches, the bit clamped firmly between his teeth; bravely he tries to hold the wagon back.

There is a large tree on the right and Tom circles the lead team off the rough road and lodges the right front wagon wheel against the tree. It holds! The wagon stops! Black-Man rises to his feet, trembling all over.

When people speak of horse sense, I know from experiences like this, just what they're talking about.

Douglas is a friendly little city and we settle into it comfortably. One morning Tom and I are drinking coffee and a man rides up to our kitchen door. Jess Cook, an old friend of Tom's from Carlsbad, now a deputy sheriff, is stationed at a nearby Diamond A camp. I pour him a cup of coffee. He appears terribly nervous about something.

Glancing at my big stomach — our baby is due any day — and gulping the strong coffee, he squares his shoulders and says, "Tom, I have a warrant for your arrest."

Tom is a beautifully made man, six feet two in height. His

eyes are a deep blue, normally. Sometimes they seem to be the blue of cold steel. Coldly, he says, "What charge?"

"Cattle stealing."

"I refuse to be taken. First, I do not own any cattle. Second, I sold what cattle I had six months ago. Finish your coffee, Jess. Our visit's over and if the Diamond As want me, you're going to need some help."

Tom fills his cup with black coffee and walks out into our back yard.

Jess Cook runs after him.

"Tom, look here. I *saw* those cattle. The brands are just beginning to peel. Now we both know that a brand is completely peeled in five weeks. If we show that you sold them six months ago, maybe they'll throw the case out of court."

That same morning in Hart's Cafe, Stewart Hunt, an influential rancher in Mexico and the surrounding area, hears of Tom's arrest and runs his horse right into our yard.

"Tom, I'm going along for the ride — any objections?"

Stewart Hunt and Tom have something in common: neither one has ever been an employee of the Diamond A Outfit and, although Hunt is much older than Tom, they are fast friends.

They go to Hachita but the case never makes it to the courtroom and Tom's only brush with the law is cancelled before it has a chance to do him any harm.

CHAPTER SEVENTEEN

HOME ON THE BORDER

Tom comes in from the corrals with a handful of wild buttercups for Hazel Marie. She puts them in a jelly jar on the table. They are beautiful. Tom has sold the Gypsum contract and we await the arrival of our new baby. Then it's back to our home on the border.

Pancho Villa's threats ring loud and clear and the Victoria Land and Cattle Company hasn't made us feel exactly welcome in Rancher's Paradise, as Tom first called it.

"I don't want any more children after this baby," I explain, "neither do I want to go back to the border. Life's just too dangerous there — not to mention there are no schools within miles of us."

Tom reaches over and firmly takes my hand in his. "I agree about no more children. But I want a son to carry the name Pendelton."

Early next morning I awaken Tom and he springs out of bed, hurriedly pulling on his levis and boots. "Sweetheart, I'll be right back with the doctor. You keep our baby in the cradle until I return. Promise?"

He runs to the corral and saddles Chester, my saddle horse. Daylight is breaking. The sun gives a faint golden glimmer in the East.

Horses are quick to detect fear in their riders and Chester snorts and lays his ears back just as Tom hits the saddle. Chester begins to buck and pitch around the corral. I hear Tom's voice plainly from inside the house.

"Chester, you old son of a bitch! What the devil's wrong?" One moment and a few last bucks later, I see Tom and Chester fly by the house, swift as the wind.

Laddie
on Blue Darter

Hazel Marie
on Crappie

Our baby, a boy, is born August 13, 1917. We name him after his two grandfathers, George for Tom's father and Edwin for my father, Edwin Bass, but I call him Laddie.

In two weeks our wagon is loaded again and we're returning to our claim in Grant County. We can't file on this land of ours because it has never been surveyed.

Now the border country of New Mexico is almost completely lawless, all the men wear guns all of the time.

Tom wears his 45 sixshooter with a belt full of cartridges buckled around his waist and on his saddle he carries a 30-30 Winchester.

The lobo's mournful howl and the barking of the coyotes awaken us early in the morning. Sometimes the coyotes sneak up near the chicken house and grab a chicken or two as the chickens leave the roost.

I learn how to pick up a six shooter and take careful aim. What woman will not fight for her chickens — especially when they're Rhode Island Reds?

Tom buys more cattle, some of which are well bred, others among them all colors. We buy Hereford bulls.

Our brand is PEN, our ear mark, under crop the left and swallow fork the right, like so:
This brand has been in existence since 1896. Soon we drop the "E." The screw worms, poisonous to the cattle, lay eggs on the newly branded ones and when these worms hatch, they go right into the brand. They're extremely poisonous.

One day we find out Alice Parker and her husband Bill have been murdered. The Parkers have a ranch about 20 miles from us and one morning when they're returning to their house from the corral with their milk, their Mexican hired hand shoots them both with Bill's 30-30 Winchester.

Then the Mexican and his wife saddle two of Bill's best saddle horses, take his rifle and ammunition and head straight for the Mexican border.

We bury Alice and Bill that afternoon.

Later on, a band of heavily armed cowboys go on a hunting trip to Mexico. Tom gives one of the men, Dink Parker, his spy glasses and they go off down the trail into Mexico where deer, antelope and wild berries are plentiful. When they return from this hunting trip in about ten days no questions are asked, but we know justice has been done.

Sometimes we have to take the law into our own hands.

Some months later another hunter's party came down hard on another bunch of fugitives. The hunters returned home with dried beef, wild strawberries and the heart of the mescale plant. Among the articles stolen were a pair of pants and a sack both made from finely dressed cowhide.

The fugitives retaliated by slipping across the border, stealing horses and robbing a home. They split a feather bed tick cover and stuffed it full of sheets, pillow cases, towels, clothing, pots and pans.

The border feuds are endless. Strange, that in these deep purple mountains, the recesses and rocky crevices of the Sierra Madre, so many unpeaceful acts are perpetrated on both sides, Mexican and Anglo.

Beauty lasts, peace does not.

CHAPTER EIGHTEEN

ROUGH CREEK

Two Mexicans from across the border build our home on Rough Creek made of soft grey lavender stone. Two large oak trees shade the front yard. Our yard fence is ocotillo; the slender stalks take root, form a dense stickery wall, and in a single spring they will go into full bloom. We place them close together so neither chicken nor pig can slip through. Our corral is made of cut cedar staves.

One day Tom and I are branding some calves. He moves the forge near the fence and asks me to do the heating of the irons even though I've never done it before.

"You keep the branding irons hot," he says, "and hand them through the fence to me. — Iron please."

I pick up an iron.

It is not bright red, it is white and its head falls off, plop, on the ground.

"My-good-God-all-mighty," Tom shouts, "you've burned them all up!"

That afternoon we use wagon rods to make more branding irons.

Tom saddle-breaks the three- and four-year-old broncs and we have a fine breed of horses. Some of the young saddle-broke broncs sell for $60.00 and up. Tom trades them for cows, lumber and other necessities.

One of his trades results in eighty head of domestic hogs which run wild in the mountains. Capturing the grown ones for fattening is an exciting and dangerous business because their tusks are two inches long and are unsparingly vicious.

When we go out to mark our baby pigs, we take Smugglers Trail which was used by the bandits who way-laid the gold trains coming from Mexico to the U.S. and laden mules with the gold and silver from the mines.

The trail is too steep, especially for the children who have come along for the day, to take any chances.

"Get down," Tom says, "We'll walk behind our horses and hold to their tails."

After the difficult climb, we sight an old sow and a bunch of piglets. The sow gives a funny signal to her babies and they are off and running, dodging trees and bushes. Tom leans over in his saddle, grabs three or four pigging strings from his belt, puts them between his teeth and races up beside the fleeing sow and her pigs. Then he springs from the saddle, grabs a little pig and ties it. The little pigs are swift on foot. Our dog Jack runs up next to Tom's horse and in no time at all he figures out what Tom's doing. Jack grabs a little pig with his front paws, presses his head firmly down on its body and Tom comes along and ties it tighter than a hatband.

My job's to ride by the running sow, never letting her get out of sight. But a sow's smart, she'll hide in the thick brush or in the high rocks of the hillside and lay low until the danger's passed.

Tom never bothered with pigging strings after that afternoon. He took Jack instead.

Tom and I also work our cattle in the rough country where the trails are steep and the wild flowers bloom. Hazel and Laddie follow us on their ponies, Chess and Blue Darter, and the horses' hooves crush the blossoms and the air fills with prairie fragrance. We love our life on Rough Creek, and even though it's hard to make ends meet we don't mind because we're all together.

Herding goats is another story.

Tom trades the fine mares for a bunch of goats. Wool sells for sixty cents a pound.

Laddie has a beautiful little black donkey named Darkey;

Hazel Marie's donkey is called Crappie.

The day the goats arrive, both children ride out to meet Tom who's bringing them in. Suddenly Darkey runs at the goats, biting and kicking and baring his teeth. Laddie's thrown from the saddle and lands hard on his head. Tom springs from his horse and brings Laddie, unconscious, into the house. Hazel's crying.

"Mother," she says, "I wish I'd been riding Darkey. Then my little brother'd be alright."

"We better take him to the doctor in Hachita," Tom says urgently.

I am bathing Laddie's face with cold water. I ask Hazel Marie to get a suitcase and pack it. Hachita, a distance of 65 miles, is rough the whole way. Tom's face is white and haggard. We sit in the wagon not saying anything.

Suddenly, Laddie opens his eyes, raises his head and says, "Daddy, where are we going?"

Tom smiles, his voice trembling, "Home, son."

CHAPTER NINETEEN

MY PRAIRIE KNIGHT

Summer glides into fall. The Apache plume blossom which resembles a wild rose in color and perfume has faded and dropped to the ground. The soft lavender plum replaces it. The winds sweep the wild grasses. The green fades into soft gold.

Hazel Marie is five. She has her own horse and saddle. Granddad Pendleton sends her a tiny western saddle. Tom gives her a small Palomino pony.

The price of cattle is low, stock water is scarce. We are fighting a drought. Tom rides from early morning until two or three o'clock in the afternoon. Money is also scarce and hard times seem never distant.

One day Tom comes in looking weary and tired. He unsaddles and turns Star loose and we go into the house together so I can prepare his lunch. Tom takes his violin from the case and begins to play.

He plays our song, *The River Shannon* and we sing together as I make lunch.

I am dreading to break some very important news to Tom.

Earlier in the day a car drove up and a lady and a young boy came into our house. She introduced herself and her son: Mrs. Deaton from Walnut Wells. She wants me to come and teach at the Walnut Wells school. Other teachers have shied away from coming so close to the border to teach.

I want to wait and talk to Tom about accepting the position, but I'm sure he will say no.

So I accept without him.

Tom finishes lunch and I tell him Mrs. Deaton from Walnut Wells paid us a visit. He is pleased. He likes the Deaton family. Mrs. Deaton operates the post office at Walnut Wells.

Tom says, "Did she bring the mail?"

Tom Pendleton

"No, she came to offer me the Walnut Wells school. I accepted it."

Tom blows up.

"I'm the head of this family and I'll support it. I'm going to ride to Walnut Wells and explain this to Mrs. Deaton."

I'm sitting at the kitchen table picking frijole beans. Tom's blue eyes flash fire, he pushes his plate aside scornfully.

"People will think you support me. Eva, you just can't do this."

Looking into Tom's face, even though his eyes are angry, I see a twitch of his upper lip — almost trembling. I realize that I have badly wounded my Prairie Knight. I want to cry. I don't want to move to Walnut Wells to teach and the only jobs for men are with the Victoria Land and Cattle Company whose monthly wage is $30.00 plus room and board. The employees are not allowed to own a brand of cattle or horses.

However, we're in debt up to our ears and I don't see any way out but teaching.

Tom doesn't speak to me. It's our longest feud, long and lonely.

But on the third morning as daylight breaks, Tom builds a fire and sets up the coffee. A loud squawk from the chicken house and Tom reaches up to get his 30-30 from the wall, aims out the window and shoots a coyote. Then he washes his hands and pours us both a cup of coffee. We drink it black.

He sits beside me on the bed. When I look into his eyes I see the winning smile back on his face.

"God, Eva, I know neither hell nor high water can make you change your mind and I know that this separation is as tough on you as it is on me. But I also realize you're doing it for us, for the family."

He leans over, hugs me tightly and then kisses me; hungrily I return his kisses.

"After breakfast I'll saddle our horses," he says. Then his eyes really light up. "You make us a sourdough biscuit sandwich and we'll take the kids to Guadalupe Canyon and rob us a bee hive."

CHAPTER TWENTY

GRASS WIDOW

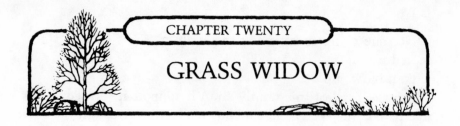

The soft golden rays of the early sunrise melt into the dark blue shadows of the majestic Sierra Madre Mountains.

The saddle horses gallop in for their *morrals* (nose bags). A handsome little bay mare is among them, flirting with Blue Darter and Star. Blue Darter is Hazel's saddle horse and he rightly deserves the name because, like a blue darter hawk, he flies in and out of a bunch of cattle. He dashes in between Star and the lady mare whirls and kicks Star.

"Godalmighty!" Tom exclaims. "That little mare is going to cause one of our saddle horses to get hurt. I guess I'll have to get rid of her."

He pours himself and me a fresh cup of hot coffee. "I'm going over the border to the Hewitt ranch," he says, "and invite them to the dance Friday night."

Walter Hewitt owns a large cattle ranch in Sonora, Mexico. You take a bad wagon road to get there and a careful car driver, dodging boulders and high middles, can just make it. There's a little summer house nearby where the mescale is served in cow horns. You sit near the banks of the Cajon Bonita River drinking liquor from a hollow cow's horn. Higher up on the banks of the Garalanda ranch, drinks are served from crystal glasses encased in sterling silver.

An all-night dance is our only social event. This year cattle prices are high, plenty of rain making fat cattle, and we've sold and delivered our steer calves and yearlings. Now it's celebration time: a big dance at the school house.

We fill the lanterns with coal oil and hang them from the rafters of the school house.

As soon as Tom leaves for the border, I start remaking my

wedding dress into a ball dress. I dye the cream satin a soft rose color. As I remake this beautiful gown, my thoughts fall into dreams of yesteryears. Happy and hazardous memories, but always of Tom. Tom out in front, loving, protecting me and the children.

Late in the afternoon I see dust south on the road to Mexico. Tom's back.

"I got Ira Sheeley to play for the dance," he tells me with wild enthusiasm.

Ira Sheeley is a famous violinist and a long-time friend of Tom's. Once when Ira was traveling in Europe with a wild west show, Queen Victoria heard of Ira's prowess with the fiddle and bow and she invited Ira to play at Buckingham Palace.

At the dance that night Ira is not wearing any fancy high-heeled boots or California pants, but a three-X Stetson and old broken huarachis. His trousers, made from an old tarpaulin, are cut and whanged (sewed by hand), the seams held together with rawhide strings. His old grey shirt is ragged, torn off sleeves at the elbow and buttonless. Tenderly he places the violin on his shoulder. The lantern hanging from the school house rafters casts a ray of light on Ira's black hair parted straight in the middle. He stands straight, too, and looks like an Indian, black hair hanging to his shoulders.

The music drifts softly through the night air. I think of the ripple of a gently flowing stream. Then like the thundering of hoof beats or the sound of stampeding cattle, the music thunders through the old Cloverdale School House. Gently it terminates into the beautiful waltz, *Good-bye My Little Sweetheart*. We are up and dancing.

An old friend of mine and Tom's is here from the eastern part of the state. Tom tells me that his friend, Dolph Teague, is embarrassed because he doesn't have his *cuttin' shoes* and Sunday suit even though he's clean and handsome in his cowboy attire.

Tom tells me to ask Dolph for a dance when a Ladies' Choice is announced and I go over and tap Dolph on the shoulder. He's dancing with a tall brunette whom I've never seen before. She releases her hold on him reluctantly.

Dolph and I dance off to the tune of a Mexican polka while the lady stares at me in a hostile manner. Then she hurries over and tags Tom.

I overhear someone say, "That's that Grass Widder from Walnut Wells. High stepper ain't she?"

The old bachelor doing the talking is Chief, formerly a member of the Al Jennings' Train Robbers Gang.

The next dance is *not* a ladies tag and Tom and I start dancing our favorite waltz, *Over The Waves*.

The Grass Widow comes waltzing toward us, tags Tom and they waltz away from me.

I remain standing, planning to tag my husband when they come back near me. Then another little lady steps in front of me and tags Tom. So, I turn and sit down beside my friend the Postmistress, Mrs. Sanford, whom we call Gammie.

"You're in trouble," she says. "I'd get up and help you but I think my foot is locked in my shoe."

"I'm afraid I don't understand."

"Well," she says, "I locked the Post Office when I left my home, put the key beneath my garter. Now, it's fallen into my slipper and since I can't walk, it has doubtless locked my foot."

I look around at the people sitting — they're all looking at me. I hear one of them say:

"That Grass Widder shore is taken to Tom Pendleton."

I realize Gammie is just trying to cheer me. My older sister Maggie is at the dance so I go over to her.

"I need help or I'm going to lock horns with that Grass Widder."

She is wearing a dress with long chiffon sleeves. Laughingly she rolls up those chiffon sleeves, goes out on the floor and tags Tom. The other little lady rushes up and tags Tom from Maggie.

I daintily step up close and tag Tom myself. My tag is not dainty, I double up my fist and sock him on the shoulder.

Tom bursts out laughing. Everyone laughs.

He says, "I hope you noticed I wasn't talking to either of

them."

"But you sure were doing some fancy footwork!"

Tom pulls me close in his arms and we do a merry whirl called the *Mexican Polka.*

The mescale flowed freely. Early in the evening I wondered where those old boys were getting their liquor and when George Godfrey and his wife arrived I heard Tom say to George: "I'm having some carburetor trouble. Come with me and see what's wrong."

I thought to myself, *They can't work on a car at night.* Soon another friend, Sim Smith came and I heard Tom say to him: "There's a sick dog outside, Sim. Let's go see how he is."

Gammie asks me to go outside with her. She wants to recover her post office key and unlock her foot. So, while Gammie is thus employed, I stroll behind the school house looking for that sick dog.

The moon shines brightly on my snow white five gallon stone vinegar jug. I remove the corn from this sick dog's mouth. Then I kick it over.

The mescale runs freely down the hill. Later on, Tom says he traded the TF mare to the vineyard owner for the five gallons.

Gammie and I return. They are doing a breakdown, or quadrille. The caller, Salty, the leader of a bunch of Diamond A cowboys from Playas Lake, rightly deserves his name. He was a cowboy who came when shootin' started. He wore high-heeled boots and his voice was like a bugle on a mountain top.

*Fellers stake your pens, tangle with them heifers
and hurry them in like men.
Salute the lovely critters, swing and let 'um go.
Climb the grape vine around 'um.
And hands do se do.*

Well, we all just galloped around. Salty's voice rang loud and clear.

Chicken in the breadpan pickin' out the dough
Granny will your dog bite—No child no
Pole money and a kicka doodle 'um
When shall the good Lord set me free.
Vaughn down the middle and twine the ladies chain
Tom Pen cut the fillies to Double diamond's range
Chase those squirrels and cut 'um right and left.

At midnight, the boys build a fire around a thirty-gallon iron kettle. We pour several packages of Arbuckle coffee into the boiling water and the ladies cut their cakes.

Shug, a handsome Diamond A cowboy, rushes up to Tom and says, "Some of the horses turned our jar over."

Tom whispers, "Who took it out from the bush I hid it in?"

"Tom, she's all gone to the last drop."

After the dance my friends always referred to the Grass Widow as "Eva's rival." But she has never given me any more trouble since that night.

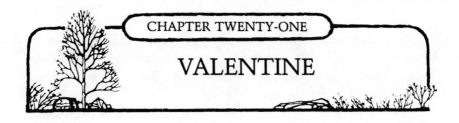

CHAPTER TWENTY-ONE

VALENTINE

When the Chairman of the Hachita School Board offers me a teaching position I have to accept, but it's so sad to leave Tom alone on the ranch with his dangerous work breaking broncs and capturing wild hogs. He feeds the hogs mescale heads and Indian corn — the meat's delicious.

Come February, the other teachers plan to go to El Paso, Texas for a four-day holiday. Tom doesn't receive mail more than once or twice a month, but two weeks before Valentine's Day I draw a heart—

To Dear Tom   My Valentine
The teachers are planning their George Washington vacation. We will have a four-day holiday.
They are going to El Paso, Texas. Were I making plans they would be to spend the four days with you. Though I know it is impossible.
The children are fine.
We love you.
Lovingly,
Eva
2.14.21

We dismiss school at 3 p.m. The day is dark, cold and cloudy. I walk out of the school house, my heart lonely, homesick for Tom. Then I see a car parked near the school house: Tom! I can't believe it, he got my Valentine!

Joyfully we head for our home on the range. Dark comes early and the car starts missing. Nearing the Hi Lonesome Ranch, slow, drizzling sleet is falling and we limp to the one-room ranch house where no one lives anymore. Tom lays posts on a large rock and drops the anvil upon the posts. He breaks them into stovewood size and starts a fire.

There is a small cook stove in the room. Tom has some canned milk, sweet potatoes and a large package of beef ribs. We place the ribs on the top grill in the oven and the sweet potatoes on the lower one.

We don't have any salt but piled against the side of the house is a block of salt for the animals. Placing a newspaper under it, Tom pounds the rock salt until we have enough to season those delicious ribs. For the sweet potatoes, we use drippings from the ribs to make a wonderful sauce.

When dark comes, we find a lantern hanging from a rafter and it is almost full of coal-oil. Near the lonely cow camp by the yard fence is a stack of prairie hay with a pitch fork sticking out of it. Tom pitches the hay into the corner of the little house and spreads a comforter over the hay and we use the other one for cover. Tom keeps the fire going all night.

At daybreak the ground is covered with snow, but Tom crawls under the car, finds what's wrong with it and does a quick repair job.

Home by 11 a.m., I cook freshly cured ham and sour-milk biscuits. We have wild cherry jam and hot coffee. Our children, Hazel Marie and George Edwin, drink hot chocolate. We love our beautiful little home on Rough Creek.

After lunch, Tom and I wash the dishes. He says, "Shall we all go to bed or ride over on Smugglers Trail?"

The children and I say, "Let's ride!"

I have a brand new saddle, Tom's Christmas present to me.

Earlier that fall I had written to Tom, "I'm so lonely and homesick. Sell the ranch and cattle. Come and get a railroad job. They pay $100 per month."

He wrote back, no.

Today, as we ride the range together, I am on Skeedadle, my beautiful cow horse and I reach over and take Tom's hand.

"Tom, don't ever let me talk you into the notion of selling our ranch and cattle. This is the finest and cleanest life in the world."

Tom presses my hand to his heart. "Don't worry, Sweetheart. I love it too. We belong on the range, you and I."

Sunday afternoon we return to Hachita.

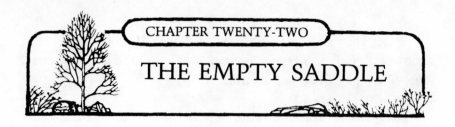

CHAPTER TWENTY-TWO

THE EMPTY SADDLE

The fall winds blow. The golden oak leaves flutter from the trees. The children and I move to Lordsburg. Hazel Marie is entering the ninth grade. I am not a town girl and I miss Tom, the lowing of the cattle, the call of the whip-poor-will so early in the morning. Lordsburg is the county seat and our ranch is 90 miles south.

Tom contracts the cattle and he and a neighbor, Jim Wolf, drive them to the railroad station at Animas, New Mexico, and wait for the buyer to show up. Rain and sleet and damp bedrolls and still the buyer doesn't come.

Tom comes to Lordsburg, he is ill with what we think is the flu. In the weeks and months that pass we learn that his sickness is tuberculosis.

I saddle Blue Darter for him, though he can't ride much any more.

I stare at that empty saddle and remember how Tom and I used to ride in the days when we were first married.

Tom drives the car to the edge of the mountains. I ride Star and lead Blue Darter to the car and then Tom and I both ride through the cattle, so he can point out the cows that need to be fed or sold. We cut those from the others and head them toward home.

Then Tom would ride back to the car, dismount from Blue Darter, take the bridle off and hang it on the saddle horn.

Tom's empty saddle makes tears trickle from my heart. I never cry out loud.

CHAPTER TWENTY-THREE

I RIDE ALONE

In 1937 Tom dies. Our friend, Sam Gass sings *Home On The Range* at the service. Our cattle are grazing by the cemetery, a soft and gentle rain falls, tears fill my heart with grief.

I am desolate. Now I ride the range alone and my memories ride with me. The mountains and trees are friends that don't talk back. They are good listeners.

My neighbors are the best people I could have close to me. When branding time comes, the men help me with the round up and branding.

The grass is short and dry, the cattle are poor. On the hillside I see a cow in labor, the forefeet of the calf protruding. I dismount, take my saddle rope from the horn and slip the loop around the tiny feet. The heifer lies tiredly on the ground among the rocks and grass.

I loop a half-hitch around the saddle horn and lean forward in the saddle.

Blue Darter steps forward, the rope tightens.

In a few moments, the calf is born. I pick it up and take it to the mother's head where she can lick it clean.

Birth, death, an empty saddle. My life alone, my memories.

CHAPTER TWENTY-FOUR

RED BIRD

After Tom's estate has been settled, I learn our cattle carry a heavy mortgage. The bank notes are due every six months.

I'm worried.

I am told confidentially and in a most matter-of-fact way that the P.N. outfit mortgage would be foreclosed come Spring. Tom and I had started the P.E.N. in 1916 in Grant County. P.E.N. was his father's brand beginning in 1894 in Eddy County. I renew the notes at the bank.

Fear sits heavily on my shoulders as I go about stocking up on ranch supplies. The supplies are all on credit.

On the way home I look out at the mountains. A bunch of blue-tassel quail scoot across the road. Then I begin to quote from the Lord's Prayer. The fear goes away and in its place I see dry yellow grass and Sago lilies blooming by the roadside in the midst of the drought.

Soon I'm singing the entire forty-eight verses of the old song *California Joe*.

The car starts to buck and stumble. A flat.

I'm wearing a coat suit with no blouse, just a jabot and I remove the coat to change the tire. The sun is setting, the sky's crimson and gold.

Suddenly a voice says, "Howdy, how about some help?"

I grab for my coat and see two Diamond A cowboys who have ridden up out of nowhere to help.

Early the next morning I drive to another bank. A small voice deep within says, "Don't cry, don't talk a lot, just ask for cheaper interest."

It works — I borrow enough money to pay back the other bank.

That night back at the ranch I free Red Bird, my favorite horse, from a bunch of tangled up barbed wire.

He is trembling all over. I use wire cutters to cut the wire and then I pat Red Bird and tell him he is free. He trots off and I start back to the house which is some distance away. Suddenly I hear the hooves of a running horse. I whirl around.

Red Bird is running toward me, mane and tail fanned out in the breeze. What a sight. When he gets up to me, he stops dead still, rubs his head back and forth against my shoulders.

Jack, my hired man, takes a picture of Red Bird and me. In the picture I show my Indian heritage. Jess Chisum. Wild horses in my blood.

I look toward a lovely purple hillside
Where the sago lilies bloom
Near the little village of Cloverdale
There stands a lonely tomb.
Nearby the cows are browsing
And the lonely nightbirds call
It is there my memory wanders
When the evening shadows fall